D0783665

RUSSELL ASH

DOUBLEDAY

BORING, BOTTY AND SPONG
A DOUBLEDAY BOOK 978 0 385 61876 2

Published in Great Britain by Doubleday,
an imprint of Random House Children's Books
A Random House Group Company

This edition published 2011

1 3 5 7 9 10 8 6 4 2

Copyright © Russell Ash, 2011
Illustrations copyright © Nigel Baines, 2011

The Random House Group Limited supports the Forest Stewardship Council (FSC®), the leading international forest certification organization. Our books carrying the FSC label are printed
on FSC®-certified paper. FSC is the only forest certification scheme endorsed by the leading
environmental organizations, including Greenpeace. Our paper procurement policy can be
found at www.randomhouse.co.uk/environment.

MIX
Paper from
responsible sources
FSC
www.fsc.org   FSC® C016897

Set in Optima

RANDOM HOUSE CHILDREN'S BOOKS
61–63 Uxbridge Road, London W5 5SA

www.kidsatrandomhouse.co.uk
www.totallyrandombooks.co.uk
www.randomhouse.co.uk

Addresses for companies within The Random House Group Limited can be found at: www.
randomhouse.co.uk/offices.htm

THE RANDOM HOUSE GROUP Limited Reg. No. 954009

A CIP catalogue record for this book is available from the British Library.

Printed and bound by CPI Group (UK) Ltd, Croydon, CR0 4YY

Introduction

This book is about names; the names of places, people and things. It combines fascinating historical facts with amazing, offbeat, weird, absurd and amusing names. It will tell you about the origins, facts and myths of our extraordinary naming traditions from all over the world and includes everything from dinosaurs to robots, from sweets to characters in well-known stories. All the names listed are real and what follows are extraordinary, funny and quirky names to make you wonder, names to make you think and names to make you laugh out loud . . .

Places

The first part of the book looks at the names of places, and covers lots of subjects, starting with the universe and the names of asteroids, which range from classic authors (Lewis Carroll) to explorers (Edmund Hillary). Then it looks at countries with the longest official names (Al-Jumhuriyyah al-Islamiyyah al-Muritaniyyah République Islamique de Mauritanie in Mauritania has 71 letters), countries named after people (Columbia), places with strange names (Booby Dingle in Herefordshire, UK and Wooloomooloo in Sydney, Australia) and nicknames for cities (The Bride of the Sea, Venice, Italy).

People

The middle section deals with people, starting with their unusual first names (Armadillo, Whalebelly). Then it moves to favourite contemporary names and their meanings, (Olivia, first used by Shakespeare in *Twelfth Night*), the most popular names throughout history and from around the world, (William is the most popular boy's name in Australia), names invented by writers (Wendy by J. M. Barrie in *Peter Pan*), celebrity baby names (Heavenly Hiraani Tiger Lily, the name of Michael Hutchence's and Paula Yates's baby), strange surnames (Baboon), unusual or amusing couples – when two people get married and join their names together (Snow-Mann) – and amusing-sounding names (Barb Dwyer, Justin Case).

Things

The final section covers the widest variety of subjects, including the meanings of dinosaur names, the names of fictional animals (Hedwig, the snowy owl from *Harry Potter*), pets' names (Molly is the most popular cat name in the UK) and food named after people (Eggs Benedict named after Samuel Benedict, a New York man-about-town and Mars Bar named for the founder of the company, Franklin Mars) to name just a few.

I hope you find this book entertaining, interesting and amusing.

Caroline Ash
Lewes, August 2011

Contents

The names of places, people and things change often, and new ones are named all the time – more than 300,000 babies are born and named throughout the world each day!

All the information in this book is, to the very best of our ability, correct at the time of going to press.

November 2011

Part 1:

Boring

PLACES

1. THE UNIVERSE

The Planets of the Solar System and Their Satellites

A name for a celestial body is known as an 'astronym', and as the universe is so large we certainly get through a lot of them! Below is a list of the planets of our solar system, along with their moons, and how they got their names – although more moons are being discovered and named all the time.

Mercury

The nearest planet to the Sun, named after the Roman messenger of the gods.

Venus

Our nearest neighbour, named after the Roman goddess of love.

Earth

The only planet not named after a Roman or Greek god; the name comes from the Old English/German words for 'ground' or 'soil'.

The Moon

From the Old English word Mōna; also related to 'month'.

Mars

The Roman god of war, because of its blood-red colour. Ancient Egyptians called it 'Her Desher', which means 'the red one'.

Phobos

The Greek god of fear.

Deimos

The Greek god of dread (Phobos's brother).

Jupiter

The largest planet is named after the most important Roman god – the king of the gods, and the god of sky and thunder (Greek name Zeus).

Metis

The first wife of Zeus/Jupiter.

Adrastea

A nymph of Crete to whose care Zeus's mother entrusted the infant Zeus.

Amalthea

A goat in some accounts, a princess of Crete in others, she suckled Zeus as a young child.

Thebe

A nymph abducted by Zeus.

Io

A nymph who was changed by Zeus into a cow to protect her from his jealous wife.

Europa

A Phoenician who was seduced by Zeus, and who also gave her name to the continent of Europe.

Ganymede

A beautiful young boy who became the
cupbearer of the Olympian gods.

Callisto

A nymph who was changed by Zeus into a bear to
protect her from his wife's jealousy.

Leda

The Queen of Sparta, who was seduced by
Zeus in the form of a swan.

Himalia

A nymph who bore three sons of Zeus.

Lysithia

Another of Zeus's many lovers.

Elara

And another.

Ananke

A daughter of Zeus and Adrastea, goddess of
fate and necessity.

Carme

The mother, by Zeus, of Britomartis, a goddess
of hunting and mountains.

Pasiphaë

The wife of Minos, mother of the minotaur.

Sinope

The daughter of the river god Asopus and Merope.

Other recently discovered and named satellites of Jupiter are:

Themisto, Euporie, Orthosie, Euanthe, Thyone, Harpalyke, Hermippe, Praxidike, Iocaste, Passithee, Chaldene, Kale, Isonoe, Aitne, Erinome, Taygete, Kalyke, Eurydome, Autonoe, Sponde, Megaclite and *Callirrhoe.*

Saturn

Saturn was the Roman name for the Greek Cronos, god of farming and the father of Zeus/Jupiter. Some of its satellites were named for Titans who, according to Greek mythology, were brothers and sisters of Saturn. The newest satellites were named for Gallic (from Gaul, or ancient France), Norse and Inuit (Eskimo) giants.

Pan
The half-human, half-goat god of pastoralism.

Atlas
A Titan who held the heavens on his shoulders.

Prometheus
A Titan who gave many gifts to humanity, including fire.

Pandora
A woman who opened the box that loosed a host of plagues upon humanity.

Janus
A two-faced Roman god who could look forward and backward at the same time.

Epimetheus
A Greek backward-looking god.

Tethys
The wife of Oceanus and mother of all rivers.

Telesto
A water nymph.

Calypso
A daughter of Atlas and paramour of Odysseus.

Dione
A sister of Cronos.

Helene
A daughter of Zeus.

Rhea
A daughter of Cronos.

Titan
The largest moon of Saturn, named
after a race of powerful Greek deities.

Hyperio
Iapetus
Mimas
Enceladus
Four of the Titans.

Phoebe
Another name for Artemis, goddess of the moon.

Other satellites of Saturn discovered since 2000 are:

Kiviuq, Ijiraq, Paaliaq, Skadi, Albiorix, Erriapo, Siarnaq, Tarvos, Mundilfari, Suttung, Thrym, Ymir, Fornjot, Loge, Kari, Surtur, Fenrir, Bestla, Aegir, Farbauti, Hati, Narvi, Bergelmir, Jarnsaxa, Hyrrokkin, Greip, Tarqeq, Skoll and *Bebhionn.*
More satellites are being discovered all the time.

Uranus

Uranus was named for the Greek god of the sky.
The astronomer William Lassell, who discovered two of Uranus's satellites in 1851, started the tradition of naming all the planet's satellites for characters in the works of William Shakespeare and Alexander Pope.

Cordelia

One of Lear's daughters in Shakespeare's *King Lear*.

Ophelia

The daughter of Polonius and fiancée of Hamlet in Shakespeare's *Hamlet*.

Bianca

The daughter of Baptista and sister of Kate in Shakespeare's *The Taming of the Shrew*.

Cressida

The title character in Shakespeare's *Troilus and Cressida*.

Desdemona

The wife of Othello in Shakespeare's *Othello*.

Juliet

The heroine of Shakespeare's *Romeo and Juliet*.

Portia
The rich heiress in Shakespeare's *The Merchant of Venice*.

Rosalind
The daughter of the banished duke in
Shakespeare's *As You Like It*.

Belinda
Umbriel
Two characters from Pope's *Rape of the Lock*.

Puck
Titania
Oberon
All characters in Shakespeare's *A Midsummer Night's Dream*.

Miranda
Ariel
Caliban
Sycorax
Prospero
Setebos
Stephano
Trinculo
Francisco
Ferdinand
All characters in Shakespeare's *The Tempest*.

Cupid
A minor character in *Timon of Athens*.

Perdita
An abandoned daughter of the King and
Queen of Sicily in *The Winter's Tale*.

Mab
A fairy queen from folklore mentioned in *Romeo and Juliet*.

Margaret
A servant in *Much Ado About Nothing*.

Neptune
This blue planet was named for the Roman god of the sea.

Naiad
A group of Greek water nymphs who were guardians
of lakes, fountains, springs and rivers.

Thalassa
Greek sea goddess.

Despina
Daughter of Neptune.

Galatea
One of the attendants of Neptune.

Larissa
A lover of Neptune.

Proteus
A Greek sea god.

Triton
The sea-god son of Poseidon/Neptune.

Nereid

This group of 50 daughters were attendants of Neptune.

Halimede
Sao
Laomedeia
Psamathe
Neso

Just a few of the Nereids.

Pluto

Pluto was demoted from planet to 'minor planet' in 2006.
It is named after the Roman god of the underworld,
who was able to render himself invisible.

Charon

The mythological boatman who ferried souls across
the river Styx to Pluto for judgement.

Nix

Charon's mother, the Greek goddess of darkness and light.

Hydra

Hercules slew this many-headed serpent.

Asteroids

The first asteroid was discovered on New Year's Day 1801, at
an observatory in Palermo, Italy, by Giuseppe Piazzi. Ceres
has since been re-classified as a 'dwarf planet' rather than an
asteroid. The first 120 asteroids discovered were given names
of goddesses from Greek and Roman mythology.

All the asteroids found since then have been numbered in the order of their discovery, but the tradition also arose that their finders had the right to name them whatever they chose. At first they were given mythological names, but as most of these had already been assigned to other heavenly bodies, astronomers then drifted through catalogues of girls' names and then, seemingly, to any other name they fancied.

The First Ten

**1. Ceres 2. Pallas 3. Juno
4. Vesta 5. Astraea 6. Hebe
7. Iris 8. Flora 9. Metis 10. Hygiea**

Named After Places

**67 Asia
1031 Arctica**
The Arctic

**1125 China
1193 Africa
1537 Transylvania**
Region; birthplace of Dracula

2830 Greenwich
Location of the Royal Observatory, London

**8088 Australia
8837 London
8849 Brighton**

Movies

10221 Kubrick

Stanley Kubrick, director of 2001: A Space Odyssey

13070 Seanconnery

Sean Connery, actor

4238 Audrey

Audrey Hepburn, actress

7032 Hitchcock

Alfred Hitchcock, film director

7037 Davidlean

David Lean, film director

9341 Gracekelly

Grace Kelly, actress

9342 Carygrant

Cary Grant, actor

Music

1034 Mozartia

Wolfgang Amadeus Mozart, composer

1815 Beethoven

Ludwig van Beethoven, composer

4147 Lennon

John Lennon, The Beatles

4148 McCartney
Paul McCartney, The Beatles

4149 Harrison
George Harrison, The Beatles

4150 Starr
Ringo Starr, The Beatles

5203 Pavarotti
Luciano Pavarotti, opera singer

7934 Sinatra
Frank Sinatra, singer

9179 Satchmo
Nickname of Louis Armstrong, jazz musician, who as a child used his 'satchel mouth' to hide his coins!

16155 Buddy
Buddy Holly, singer

17059 Elvis
Elvis Presley, singer

19383 Rolling Stones
The Rolling Stones, band

Sports

1740 Nurmi
Paavo Nurmi, Finnish runner, winner of nine Olympic gold medals

2472 Bradman
Donald Bradman, Australian cricketer

6758 Jesseowens
Jesse Owens, athlete

12373 Lancearmstrong
Lance Armstrong, Tour de France cyclist

Writers and Philosophers

2675 Tolkien

J. R. R. Tolkien, Lord of the Rings *author*

2807 Karl Marx

German father of communism

2985 Shakespeare

William Shakespeare, playwright

4370 Dickens

Charles Dickens, novelist

6223 Dahl

Roald Dahl, children's author

6440 Ransome

Arthur Ransome, author of Swallows and Amazons

6984 Lewiscarroll

Alice in Wonderland *author Lewis Carroll*

7016 Conandoyle

Arthur Conan Doyle, creator of Sherlock Holmes

7644 Cslewis

C. S. Lewis, author of The Chronicles of Narnia

11020 Orwell

George Orwell, author of 1984

25924 Douglasadams

Douglas Adams, author of The Hitchhiker's Guide to the Galaxy

Artists

3001 Michelangelo
Michelangelo Buonarroti, painter and sculptor

4511 Rembrandt
Rembrandt van Rijn, painter

5800 Pollock
Jackson Pollock, 'action' painter

6676 Monet
Claude Monet, impressionist painter

6701 Warhol
Andy Warhol, pop artist

Scientists, Explorers and Pioneers

1772 Gagarin
Russian cosmonaut Yuri Gagarin, the first man in space

2473 Heyerdahl
Thor Heyerdahl, Norwegian explorer

3130 Hillary
Edmund Hillary, one of the first mountaineers to climb Everest

3256 Daguerre
Louis Daguerre, photographic pioneer

4342 Freud
Sigmund Freud, father of psychoanalysis

6032 Nobel
Alfred Nobel, founder of the Nobel Prizes

6469 Armstrong
Neil Armstrong, Apollo 11 – first man on the moon

6470 Aldrin
Buzz Aldrin, Apollo 11 – second man on the moon

6471 Collins
Michael Collins, Apollo 11

6542 Jacquescousteau
Jacques-Yves Cousteau, marine explorer

Historical Figures

216 Kleopatra
Queen Cleopatra of Egypt

932 Hooveria
US president Herbert Hoover

3362 Khufu
Egyptian pharaoh Khufu, builder of the Great Pyramid

5102 Benfranklin
Benjamin Franklin, American scientist and statesman

5535 Annefrank
Anne Frank, who wrote a diary while hiding from the Nazis

7117 Claudius
Roman Emperor Claudius

Characters from Arthurian Legend

2041 Lancelot
Knight of the Round Table

2082 Galahad
Knight of the Round Table

2483 Guinevere
King Arthur's queen

2597 Arthur
King Arthur

2598 Merlin
Wizard at the court of King Arthur

Fictional Characters

5049 Sherlock
Sherlock Holmes, detective

5050 Doctorwatson
Dr Watson, Sherlock Holmes's companion

6042 Cheshirecat
The Cheshire Cat in Alice in Wonderland

6735 Madhatter
The Mad Hatter from Alice in Wonderland

9007 James Bond
James Bond, spy

18610 Arthurdent
Arthur Dent from The Hitchhiker's Guide to the Galaxy

29401 Asterix
Asterix, famous comic-strip character by Goscinny and Uderzo

29402 Obelix
Obélix, famous comic-strip character by Goscinny and Uderzo

2. COUNTRIES

• • • • • • • • • • • • • • • •

Countries with the Longest Official Names

It gets a bit tiring saying these countries' names in full every time, so their shorter common names are listed in brackets below.

1. Al-Jumhūriyyah al-Islāmiyyah al-Mūarītāniyyah République Islamique de Mauritanie
70 letters (Mauritania)

GIVE ME AN 'A'...

This song could take some time!

2. Al-Jamāhirīyyah al-'Arabiyyah al-Libiyyah aš-Ša'biyyah al-Ištirakiyyah al-'Uzmā

65 letters (Libya)

(As this book went to print, Libya was undergoing a revolution, so this may not be the official name by the time you read this!)

3. Al Jumhuriyya al Jazaa'iriyya al Dimuqratiyya ash Sha'biyya

50 letters (Algeria)

4. United Kingdom of Great Britain and Northern Ireland

45 letters (United Kingdom)

5.= Jumhuriyat al-Qumur al Ittihadiyah al-Islamiyah

41 letters (The Comoros)

5.= Sri Lanka Prajatantrika Samajavadi Janarajaya

41 letters (Sri Lanka)

7. República Democrática de São Tomé e Príncipe

38 letters (São Tomé and Príncipe)

8. Federation of Saint Christopher and Nevis

36 letters (St Kitts and Nevis)

9. Federal Democratic Republic of Ethiopia
35 letters (Ethiopia)

10.= Al-Mamlakah al-Urdunniyah al-Hashimiyah
34 letters (Jordan)

10.= Sathalanalat Paxathipatai Paxaxôn Lao
34 letters (Laos)

(Some official names have been transliterated from languages that do not use the Roman alphabet, which means converting text from one language system into another according to how the words sound, and their length may vary according to the method used.)

There is clearly no connection between the length of names and the longevity of the nation states that bear them as three former candidates have ceased to exist:

Socijalisticka Federativna Republika Jugoslavija
45 letters (Yugoslavia)

Soyuz Sovetskikh Sotsialisticheskikh Respublik
43 letters (USSR)

Ceskoslovenská Socialistická Republika
36 letters (Czechoslovakia)

Uruguay's official name of La República Oriental del Uruguay is sometimes given in full as the 38-letter La República de la Banda Oriental del Uruguay, which would place it in equal 6th position.

Largest Countries Named After Real People

Many countries were named after mythical characters, or saints of dubious historical authenticity – often because they were discovered on the saint's day – but these are all named after real people.

1. United States of America
Amerigo Vespucci (Italy; 1451–1512)

2. Saudi Arabia
Abdul Aziz ibn-Saud (Nejd, Saudi Arabia; 1882–1953)

3. Bolivia
Simón Bolívar (Venezuela; 1783–1830)

4. Colombia
Christopher Columbus (Italy; 1451–1506)

5. Philippines
Philip II (Spain; 1527–98)

6. Swaziland
Mswati II (Swaziland; c.1820–68)

7. Falkland Islands
Lucius Cary, 2nd Viscount Falkland (Britain; c.1610–43)

8. Mauritius

Maurice of Nassau (Prince of Orange; 1567–1625)

9. Kiribati

Thomas Gilbert (British; *fl.* 1780s)

10. Northern Mariana

Maria Theresa (Austria; 1717–80)

It is questionable whether China is named after the Emperor Chin, but if so it would rank first.

The origin of the name 'America' is also uncertain, with some authorities citing a Richard Amerike (*c.*1445–1503) as another possible source.

Some countries have lost their former names: Rhodesia, named after Cecil Rhodes, was renamed when Zambia was created from Northern Rhodesia in 1964 and Zimbabwe from Southern Rhodesia in 1980.

The Largest Countries to Have Changed Their Names in the Past 100 Years

You won't find these countries listed in your atlas (assuming it's up to date), as they have all changed their names in the last century.

Original names are in bold, current names are in italics, and the year the name was changed is in brackets.

1. Zaïre

Democratic Republic of Congo (1997)

2. Dutch East Indies
Indonesia (1945)

3. Persia
Iran (1935)

4. Tanganyika/Zanzibar
Tanzania (1964)

5. South West Africa
Namibia (1990)

6. Northern Rhodesia
Zambia (1964)

7. Burma
Myanmar (1989)

8. Ubanghi Shari
Central African Republic (1960)

9. Bechuanaland
Botswana (1966)

10. Siam
Thailand (1939)

11. Mesopotamia
Iraq (1921)

12. Southern Rhodesia
Zimbabwe (1980)

Although not a fully independent country, *Greenland* has been officially known as Kalaallit Nunaat since 1979, and could be considered number two in this list as it is larger than Indonesia.

The Largest Countries Whose Names Are Included in Those of Their Capital City

1. Brasília, Brazil
2. Mexico City, Mexico
3. Algiers, Algeria
4. Guatemala City, Guatemala
5. Tunis, Tunisia
6. Santo Domingo, Dominican Republic
7. Singapore, Singapore
8. Panama City, Panama
9. Kuwait, Kuwait
10. Bissau, Guinea Bissau

In some instances, the city took its name from the country, while in others it was the other way round. Among smaller countries exhibiting this phenomenon are Djibouti (Djibouti), Luxembourg (Luxembourg), São Tomé (São Tomé and Príncipe), Andorra la Vella (Andorra), Monaco (Monaco), San Marino (San Marino) and Vatican City (Vatican City).

US State Nicknames

The United States of America has a very literal name, as it is a country made up of 50 different states, each of which operates with its own governments and local laws, but all of which are united under one federal government. Each state has its own official name, but they have also picked up a few nicknames over the years . . .

Alabama
The Yellowhammer State; the Heart of Dixie;
the Camellia State

Alaska
The Last Frontier; the Mainland State

Arizona
The Grand Canyon State; the Copper State; the Apache State

Arkansas
The Natural State; Land of Opportunity;
the Razorback State; the Bear State

California
The Golden State

Colorado
The Centennial State; Colorful Colorado

Connecticut
The Constitution State; the Nutmeg State

Delaware
The First State; the Diamond State;
the Blue Hen State; Small Wonder

Florida
The Sunshine State; the Everglade State

Georgia
The Peach State; the Empire of the South;
the Goober State

Hawaii
The Aloha State; the Pineapple State

Idaho
The Gem State; the Spud State

Illinois
The Prairie State; the Land of Lincoln

Indiana
The Hoosier State

Iowa
The Hawkeye State; the Corn State

Kansas
The Sunflower State; the Jayhawker State; Salt of the Earth

Kentucky
The Bluegrass State

Louisiana
The Pelican State; the Sugar State; the Creole State

Maine
The Pine Tree State

Maryland
The Old Line State; the Free State

Massachusetts
The Bay State; the Old Colony

Michigan
The Great Lakes State; the Wolverine State

Minnesota

The North Star State; the Gopher State;
Land of 10,000 Lakes; the Bread and Butter State

Mississippi

The Magnolia State; Big Sky Country

Missouri

The Show Me State; the Bullion State

Montana

The Treasure State; Big Sky Country

Nebraska

The Cornhusker State; the Beef State

Nevada

The Silver State; the Battle Born State; the Sagebrush State

New Hampshire

The Granite State

New Jersey

The Garden State

New Mexico

The Land of Enchantment; the Sunshine State

New York

The Empire State

North Carolina

The Tar Heel State; the Old North State

North Dakota

The Peace Garden State; the Flickertail State;
The Roughrider State

Ohio

The Buckeye State; Modern Mother of Presidents

Oklahoma

The Sooner State

Oregon

The Beaver State; the Sunset State

Pennsylvania

The Keystone State; the Quaker State

Rhode Island

The Ocean State; the Plantation State;
Little Rhody

South Carolina

The Palmetto State

South Dakota

The Coyote State; the Mount Rushmore State;
the Sunshine State

Tennessee

The Volunteer State; the Big Bend State

Texas

The Lone Star State

Utah

The Beehive State; the Mormon State

Vermont
The Green Mountain State

Virginia
The Old Dominion State; the Mother of Presidents

Washington
The Evergreen State; the Chinook State

West Virginia
The Mountain State; the Panhandle State

Wisconsin
The Badger State; America's Dairyland

Wyoming
The Equality State; the Cowboy State

State Capitals

Montgomery, Alabama
US general Richard Montgomery

Juneau, Alaska
Joseph Juneau, gold prospector

Denver, Colorado
General James W. Denver

Annapolis, Maryland
Princess, later Queen Anne

Lansing, Michigan
John Lansing (1754–1829)

St Paul, Minnesota
St Paul

Jackson, Mississippi
Andrew Jackson, 7th president

Jefferson City, Missouri
Thomas Jefferson, 3rd president

Carson City, Nevada
Kit Carson (1809–68), frontiersman

Trenton, New Jersey
William Trent, merchant

Albany, New York
Duke of Albany, a title of the Duke of York (later James II)

Raleigh, North Carolina
Sir Walter Raleigh

Bismarck, North Dakota
German chancellor Otto von Bismarck (1815–98), in gratitude
for financial aid in building the railroad there

Columbus, Ohio
Christopher Columbus

Harrisburg, Pennsylvania
John Harris, Quaker founder of the city

Pierre, South Dakota
Fur trapper Pierre Choteau

Nashville, Tennessee
American general Francis Nash (1742–77)

Austin, Texas
Stephen F. Austin (1793–1836), state colonizer

Charleston, West Virginia
Charles, father of founder George Clendenin

Madison, Wisconsin
James Madison, 4th president

US States Named After People

Some of the states also take their official
names from real people . . .

Delaware
Lord De La Warr

District of Columbia
Christopher Columbus

Georgia
King George II

Hawaii
Hawaii Loa, legendary discoverer of the islands

Louisiana
King Louis XIV

Maryland
Queen Henrietta Maria

New Mexico
Aztec god Mexitli

New York
James II, when Duke of York

North/South Carolina
Charles IX of France/Charles I & II of England

Pennsylvania
William Penn

Virginia/West Virginia
Virgin Queen Elizabeth I

Washington
George Washington

3. CITIES AND TOWNS

● ● ● ● ● ● ● ● ● ● ● ● ● ●

Most Common Place Names in Great Britain

The top 10 place names in Great Britain account for 1,170 different locations. Are any of them close to where you live?

1. Newton
2. Blackhill/Black Hill
3. Castlehill/Castle Hill
4. Mountpleasant/Mount Pleasant
5. Woodside/Wood Side
6. Newtown/New Town
7. Burnside
8. Greenhill/Green Hill
9. Woodend/Wood End
10. Beacon Hill

Source: *Ordnance Survey*

These entries include the names of towns, villages and other inhabited settlements, as well as woods, hills and named locations, but exclude combinations of these names with others (Newton Abbot and Newton-le-Willows, for example, are not counted with the Newtons).

Most Common Place Names in the USA

1. Midway
2. Fairview
3. Oak Grove
4. Five Points
5. Riverside
6. Pleasant Hill
7. Mount Pleasant
8. Bethel
9. Centerville
10. New Hope
11. Liberty
12. Oakland
13. Union
14. Pleasant Valley
15. Salem
16. Georgetown
17. Springfield
18. Franklin
19. Greenville
20. Arlington

Springfield was chosen as the location for *The Simpsons*, as it could be any one of 67 – its location is never identified, and the programme makers have fun disguising where it is with misleading information; for example, it seems to be in the middle of the USA and has a desert, but somehow also has a coastline! When *The Simpsons Movie* was launched in 2007, Springfields across the USA competed to host the event; the competition was won by Springfield, Vermont.

Strange Place Names in the UK

Ab Kettleby, Leicestershire
Adventurer's Land, Cambridgeshire
Ainderby Quernhow, North Yorkshire
America, Shropshire
Anthill Common, Hampshire
The Apes Hall, Cambridgeshire
Asick Bottom, North Yorkshire

Assloss, East Ayrshire
Bachelor's Bump, East Sussex
Backside, Banffshire
Bare, Lancashire
Barripper, Cornwall
Barton in the Beans, Leicestershire
Beacon's Bottom, Buckinghamshire
Bean, Kent
Bedlam, Dorset
Beeby, Leicestershire
Beer, Devon
Beeswing, Kirkcudbrightshire
Black Dog, Devon
Blowup Nose, Grampian
Blubberhouses, North Yorkshire
Bobbing, Kent
The Bog, Shropshire
Bogend, Nottinghamshire
Booby Dingle, Herefordshire
Boothby Graffoe, Lincolnshire
Booze, North Yorkshire
Bottom Flash, Cheshire
Bottomhead, Aberdeenshire
Bottom House, Staffordshire
Bottoms, Cornwall
Box, Wiltshire

Brawl, Highland
Brill, Buckinghamshire
Broad Laying, Hampshire
Broadbottom, Greater Manchester
Broughton Poggs, Oxfordshire
Brownyside, Northumberland
Bumbles Green, Essex
Bunny, Nottinghamshire
Burnt Houses, Durham
Burpham, West Sussex
Buttock, Lancashire
Cackle Street, East Sussex
California, Norfolk
Canada, Hampshire
Carlton Scroop, Lincolnshire
Catbrain, Gloucestershire
Catsick Hill, Leicestershire
Catchems Corners, West Midlands
Chaldon Herring, Dorset
Chalk, Kent
Chemistry, Cheshire
Chew Magna, Somerset
Child's Ercall, Shropshire
Chimney, Oxfordshire
Chipchase Strothers, Northumberland
Christmaspie, Surrey

Clock Face, Merseyside
Cockayne Hatley, Bedfordshire
Coldblow, Dyfed
Cold Christmas, Hertfordshire
Cop Street, Kent
Coven, Staffordshire
Crackpot, North Yorkshire
Crank, Merseyside
Crazies Hill, Berkshire
Crimble, Greater Manchester
Crook of Devon, Kinross-shire
Cuckoo's Nest, Cheshire
The Darling, Staffordshire
Dead Cow Point, Devon
Dimple, Derbyshire
Dirty Gutter, Staffordshire
Dishes, Orkney
Diss, Norfolk
Dog Kennel, Oxfordshire
Dog Village, Devon
Donkey Town, Surrey
Doomsday Green, West Sussex
Dreadnought, Norfolk
Droop, Dorset
Duck End, Bedfordshire
Duck End, Essex

Dull, Perthshire
Eagle, Lincolnshire
Egypt, Hampshire
Eye, Suffolk
Fatfield, Tyne and Wear
Fattahead, Aberdeenshire
Flash, Staffordshire
Football Hole, Northumberland
The Forties, Derbyshire
Foul End, Warwickshire
Four Forks, Somerset
Four Throws, Kent
Friendly, West Yorkshire
Frolic, Northumberland
Giggleswick, North Yorkshire
Glutton, Highland
Gog Magog Hills, Cambridgeshire
Golden Fleece, Cumberland
Good Easter, Essex
Goonbell, Cornwall
Goosey, Oxfordshire
Great Fryup Dale, North Yorkshire
Great Intake, Cumberland
Great Snoring, Norfolk
Gweek, Cornwall
Halfpenny, Cumberland

Ham, Kent
Headroom, Aberdeenshire
Hearts Delight, Kent
Hen Poo, Scottish Borders
Hey, Lancashire
Hole in the Wall, Herefordshire
Hollywood, Staffordshire
Honeystreet, Wiltshire
Hopton Wafers, Shropshire
Howle, Shropshire
Huish Champflower, Somerset
Hungry Law, *Scottish Borders*
Idle, West Yorkshire
Indian Queens, Cornwall
Inkpen, Berkshire
Jumble, Derbyshire
Jump, South Yorkshire
Junk, Shetland
Kingston Bagpuize, Oxfordshire
Knock, Cumberland
Knockerdown, Derbyshire
Knotting, Bedfordshire
Knotty Ash, Merseyside
Land of Nod, Hampshire
Landshipping, Dyfed
Leaves Green, Greater London

Leek, Staffordshire
Lickey End, Worcestershire
Little Snoring, Norfolk
Locksbottom, Greater London
Loggerheads, Staffordshire
London Apprentice, Cornwall

Looe, Cornwall
The Loons, Orkney
Loose, Kent
Loose Bottom, East Sussex
Lost, Aberdeenshire

Lover, Wiltshire
Lowda, Cumberland
Lower Slaughter, Gloucestershire
Lower Upham, Hampshire
Lucker, Northumberland
Lucky Hole, Cornwall
Lucky Scalp, Fife
Lumps of Garryhorn, Dumfriesshire
Luxulyan, Cornwall
Lyne Down, Herefordshire
Maggieknockater, Moray
Maggots End, Essex
Matching Tye, Essex
Mavis Grind, Shetland
Melbury Bubb, Dorset
Messing, Essex
Metal Bridge, Cumberland
Middle Wallop, Hampshire
Minting, Lincolnshire
Mockbeggar, Kent
Mockham Down Gate, Devon
Moon's Moat, Worcestershire
Moscow, Cumberland
Mousehole, Cornwall
Mow Cop, Staffordshire
Mucking, Essex

Mudd, Cheshire
Mudford Sock, Somerset
Muggleswick, County Durham
Mumbles, Swansea
Nasty, Hertfordshire
Nether Wallop, Hampshire
Netherthong, West Yorkshire
New Invention, Staffordshire
New York, Northumberland
Nicky Nook, Lancashire
No Man's Land, West Sussex
Noah's Ark, Oxfordshire
Nobottle, Northamptonshire
North Piddle, Worcestershire
Odd Down, Somerset
Ogle, Northumberland
Oh Me Edge, Northumberland
Old, Northamptonshire
Old Wives Lees, Kent
Oliver's Battery, Hampshire
Outcast, Lancashire
Over, Cambridgeshire
Pant, Shropshire
Pantside, Monmouthshire
Pennycomequick, Devon
Pett Bottom, Kent

Pill, Somerset
Pink Green, Worcestershire
Pity Me, Durham
Plucks Gutter, Kent
Plush, Dorset
Polyphant, Cornwall
Pratts Bottom, Greater London
Praze-an-Beeble, Cornwall
Prospect, Cumberland
Quaking Houses, Durham
Queen Camel, Somerset
Quick, West Yorkshire
Ramsey Forty Foot, Huntingdonshire
Raw, North Yorkshire
Readymoney, *Cornwall*
Rest and Be Thankful, Argyll and Bute
Retire, Cornwall
Rhodesia, Nottinghamshire
Rhude, Devon
Robin Hood, Lancashire
Rotten End, Essex
Rubery, West Midlands
Ruyton-XI-Towns, Shropshire
Ryme Intrinseca, Dorset
Sale, Cheshire
Salt, Staffordshire

Seal, Kent
Selling, Kent
Send, Surrey
Sheepwash, Northumberland
Sheepy Parva, Leicestershire
Shelf, West Yorkshire
The Shoe, Wiltshire
Sid, Devon
Six Mile Bottom, Cambridgeshire
Skinner's Bottom, Cornwall
Slack, West Yorkshire
Solomon's Tump, Gloucestershire
Sound, Cheshire
Spacey Houses, West Yorkshire
Spital in the Street, Lincolnshire
Spital Tongues, Northumberland
Splatt, Cornwall
Splott, Glamorgan
Square and Compass, Pembrokeshire
Steep, Hampshire
Sticker, Cornwall
Sunk Island, East Yorkshire
Swallow, Lincolnshire
Swan Bottom, Buckinghamshire
Swine, East Yorkshire
Tally Ho, Devon

Thong, Kent
Thrashbush, Lanarkshire
Tiptoe, Hampshire
Toe Head, Western Isles
Toller Porcorum, Dorset
Tongue, Sutherland
Tongue of Gangsta, Orkney
Triangle, West Yorkshire
Trumpet, Herefordshire
Tumby Woodside, Lincolnshire
Twelveheads, Cornwall
Twenty, Lincolnshire
Twice Brewed, Northumberland
Twizell, Northumberland
Ugley, Essex
Unthank, Cumberland
Upend, Cambridgeshire
Upper Up, Gloucestershire
Upperthong, West Yorkshire
Vinegar Hill, Monmouthshire
Washaway, Cornwall
Wasps Nest, Lincolnshire
Weedon Lois, Northamptonshire
Weeley, Essex
Wendy, Cambridgeshire
Weston-under-Lizard, Staffordshire

Westward Ho!, Devon[1]
Wigtwizzle, Yorkshire
Wigwig, Shropshire
Wombleton, Yorkshire
Womenswold, Kent
Yelling, Huntingdonshire

Strange Place Names of the World

Canada

**Aachikaayusaakaasich
Portage,** Quebec
Asbestos, Quebec
Badger, Newfoundland
Baldy Hughes, British Columbia
Belly River, Alberta
Blow Me Down, Newfoundland
Brilliant, British Columbia
Button, Manitoba
Cape Onion, Newfoundland
Chicken, Saskatchewan
Chin, Alberta
Cranberry Portage, Manitoba

Named after the 1855 novel *Westward Ho!* by Charles
Kingsley. Saint-Louis-du-Ha! Ha!, Quebec, Canada, is the
only other place with an exclamation mark in its name.

Economy, Nova Scotia
Ecum Secum, Nova Scotia
Finger, Manitoba
Funnybone Lake, Ontario
Goblin, Newfoundland
Gore, Nova Scotia
Head-Smashed-In Buffalo Jump, Alberta
Leading Tickles West, Newfoundland
Likely, British Columbia
Little Britain, Ontario
Loos, British Columbia
Medicine Hat, Alberta
Mosquito, Newfoundland
Nonsuch, Manitoba
Nowhere Island, Ontario
Nunavut Belcher Islands, Nova Scotia
Old Sweat, Nova Scotia
Pooch Lake, Ontario
Pooh Lake, Ontario
Poopoo Creek, British Columbia
Punkeydoodles Corners, Ontario
Seven Persons, Alberta
Skookumchuck, British Columbia
Spuzzum, British Columbia
Ta Ta Creek, British Columbia
Zigzag Island, Nova Scotia

Bacon, Indiana
Bear, Delaware
Beauty, Kentucky
Beaverdale, Pennsylvania
Bee Lick, Kentucky
Beebeetown, Iowa
Best, Texas
Big Rock Candy Mountain, Vermont
Bigfoot, Texas
Bingo, Maine
Bird-in-Hand, Pennsylvania
Birdseye, Indiana
Black Gnat, Kentucky
Bottom, North Carolina
Bountiful, Utah
Bowlegs, Oklahoma
Brainy Boro, New Jersey
Bread Loaf, Vermont
Bugscuffle, Tennessee
Bumble Bee, Arizona
Buttermilk, Kansas
Camel Hump, Wyoming
Carefree, Arizona
Celebration, Florida

Cheesequake, New Jersey
Chicken, Alaska
Chocolate Bayou, Texas
Chunky, Mississippi
Concrete, North Dakota
Coward, South Carolina
Difficult, Tennessee
Dinkytown, Minnesota

Dinosaur, Colorado
Dog Walk, Kentucky
Drain, Oregon
Eek, Alaska
Eighty Eight, Kentucky
Elephant Butte, New Mexico
Embarrass, Wisconsin
Enough, Missouri
Fish Haven, Idaho
Flat, Texas
Fleatown, Ohio
Fly, Ohio
Foggy Bottom, Washington, DC
Friendly, West Virginia
Frostproof, Florida
Goodfood, Mississippi
Goose Pimple Junction, Virginia
Gravity, Iowa
Greasy, Oklahoma
Gripe, Arizona
Gunbarrel, Colorado
Ham Lake, Minnesota
Happy Camp, California
Happyland, Connecticut
Hardscrabble, Delaware
Hazard, Kentucky

Hippo, Kentucky
Horseheads, New York
Hot Coffee, Mississippi
Hourglass, Delaware
Humansville, Missouri
Humptulips, Washington
Hungry Horse, Montana
Ideal, Georgia
Jackpot, Nevada
Kissimmee, Florida
Left Hand, West Virginia
Lick Fork, Virginia
Lickskillet, Ohio
Lovely, Kentucky
Luck Stop, Kentucky
Magic City, Idaho
Mammoth, West Virginia
Mexican Hat, Utah
Mexican Water, Arizona
Monkey's Eyebrow, Kentucky
Neversink, New York
No Name, Colorado
Noone, New Hampshire
Normal, Illinois
Oatmeal, Texas
Oblong, Illinois

Oddville, Kentucky
Okay, Oklahoma
Oniontown, Pennsylvania
Ordinary, Kentucky
Panic, Pennsylvania
Parachute, Colorado
Paradise, Michigan
Parrot, Kentucky
Peculiar, Missouri
Picnic, Florida
Pie Town, New Mexico
Pigeon, Michigan
Pocket, Virginia
Porcupine, South Dakota
Possum Trot, Kentucky
Puzzletown, Pennsylvania
Rabbit Shuffle, North Carolina
Sandwich, Massachusetts
Savage, Minnesota
Shoofly, North Carolina
Shoulderblade, Kentucky
Smileyberg, Kansas
Sod, West Virginia
Spuds, *Florida*
Squirrel Hill, Pennsylvania
Stiffknee Knob, North Carolina

Success, Missouri
Sugar City, Idaho
Surprise, Arizona
Sweet Lips, Tennessee
Tea, South Dakota
Thunderbolt, Georgia
Tingle, New Mexico
Toad Suck, Arkansas
Toast, North Carolina
Tortilla Flat, Arizona
Trout, Louisiana
Turkey, Texas
Turkey Scratch, Arkansas
Two Egg, Florida
Umpire, Arkansas
Viper, Kentucky
Waterproof, Louisiana
Weed, California
West Thumb, Wyoming
What Cheer, Iowa
Why, Arizona
Y, Alaska
Zigzag, Oregon

Rest of the World

Banana, Australia
Bitey Bitey, Pitcairn Island
Boom, Belgium
Burrumbuttock, Australia
Christmas Island, Australia
Die, France
Ed, Sweden
Egg, Austria
Humpty Doo, Australia
Ii, Finland
Innaloo, Australia
John Catch a Cow, Pitcairn Island
Nar Nar Goon, Australia
Rottenegg, Austria
Silly, Belgium
Town of Seventeen Seventy, Australia
Two Boars Roll, Pitcairn Island
Useless Loop, Australia
Wagga Wagga, Australia
Wedding, Germany
Wooloomooloo, Australia
Worms, Germany

Longest Place Names in the World

(including single-word, hyphenated and multiple-word names)

1. Krung Thep Mahanakhon Amon Rattanakosin Mahinthara Ayuthaya Mahadilok Phop Noppharat Ratchathani Burirom Udomratchaniwet Mahasathan Amon Piman Awatan Sathit Sakkathattiya Witsanukam Prasit

(168 letters)

It means 'The city of angels, the great city, the eternal jewel city, the impregnable city of God Indra, the grand capital of the world endowed with nine precious gems, the happy city, abounding in an enormous Royal Palace that resembles the heavenly abode where reigns the reincarnated god, a city given by Indra and built by Vishnukarn'. When the poetic name of Bangkok, capital of Thailand, is used, it is usually abbreviated to 'Krung Thep' (city of angels).

2. Taumatawhakatangihanga-koauauotamateaturipukakapikimaun-gahoronukupokaiwhenuakitanatahu

(85 letters)

This is the longer version (the other has a mere 83 letters) of the Maori name of a hill in New Zealand. It translates as 'The place where Tamatea, the man with the big knees, who slid, climbed and swallowed mountains, known as land-eater, played on the flute to his loved one'.

3. Gorsafawddachaidraigddanheddo-gleddollônpenrhynareurdrae-thceredigion

(67 letters)

A name contrived by the Fairbourne Steam Railway, Gwynedd, North Wales, for publicity purposes and in order to outdo its rival, number four in this list. It means 'The Mawddach station and its dragon teeth at the Northern Penrhyn Road on the golden beach of Cardigan Bay'.

4. Llanfairpwllgwyngyllgogerychwyrnd-robwllllantysiliogogogoch

(58 letters)

This is the place in Gwynedd famed for the length of its railway tickets. It means 'St Mary's Church in the hollow of the white hazel near to the rapid whirlpool of the church of St Tysilo near the Red Cave'. Questions have been raised about its authenticity, since its official name comprises only the first 20 letters, and the full name appears to have been invented in the 19th century by a local tailor as a hoax.

5. El Pueblo de Nuestra Señora la Reina de los Ángeles de la Porciúncula

(57 letters)

The site of a Franciscan mission and the full Spanish name of Los Angeles; it means 'The town of Our Lady the Queen of the Angels of the Little Portion'. Nowadays it is customarily known by its initial letters, LA, making it also one of the shortest-named cities in the world.

6. Chargoggagoggmanchauga goggchaubunagungamaug

(43 letters)

America's second longest place name is this lake near
Webster, Massachusetts. Its Indian name, loosely translated, is
claimed to mean 'You fish on your side, I'll fish on mine, and
no one fishes in the middle'. It is said to be pronounced
'Char-gogg-a-gogg [pause] man-chaugg-a-gog [pause]
chau-bun-a-gung-a-maug'. This is, however, an invented
extension of its real name (Chabunagungamaug, or
'boundary fishing place'), devised in the 1920s by
Larry Daly, the editor of the *Webster Times*.

7.= Lower North Branch Little Southwest Miramichi

(40 letters)

Canada's longest place name – a short river in New Brunswick.

7.= Villa Real de la Santa Fé de San Francisco de Asis

(40 letters)

The full Spanish name of Santa Fe, New Mexico, translates as,
'Royal city of the holy faith of St Francis of Assisi'.

9. Te Whakatakanga-o-te-ngarehu-o-te-ahi-a-Tamatea

(38 letters)

The Maori name of Hammer Springs, New Zealand; like
the second name in this list, it refers to a legend of Tamatea,
explaining how the springs were warmed by 'the falling of the

cinders of the fire of Tamatea'. Its name is variously written either hyphenated or as a single word.

10. Meallan Liath Coire Mhic Dhubhghaill
(32 letters)

The longest multiple-word name in Scotland, a place near Aultanrynie, Highland, alternatively spelled Meallan Liath Coire Mhic Dhughaill (30 letters).

Longest Place Names in the UK

(Single and hyphenated names only)

1. Gorsafawddachaidraigdda nheddogleddollônpenrhyn- areurdraethceredigion
Gwynned, Wales
(67 letters)

2. Llanfairpwllgwyngyllgogerychwyrn- drobwllllantysiliogogogoch
Anglesey, Wales
(58 letters)

3. Sutton-under-Whitestonecliffe
North Yorkshire, England
(27 letters)

4. Llansantffraid-ym-mechain
Powys, Wales
(23 letters)

5. Llanfihangel-yng-Ngwynfa
Powys, Wales
(22 letters)

6.= Llanfihangel-y-Creuddyn
Ceredigion, Wales
(21 letters)

6.= Llanfihangel-y-traethau
Gwynedd, Wales
(21 letters)

8. Cottonshopeburnfoot
Northumberland, England
(19 letters)

9.= Blakehopeburnhaugh
Northumberland, England
(18 letters)

9.= Coignafeuinternich
Invernesshire, Scotland
(18 letters)

Longest Place Names in the USA

(single word names only)

1. Chargoggagoggmanchauggag-oggchaubunagungamaugg
Massachusetts (45 letters)

2. Nunathloogagamiutbingoi Dunes
Alaska (23 letters)

3.= Kleinfeltersville
Pennsylvania (17 letters)
3.= Mooselookmeguntic
Maine (17 letters)
5.= Chancellorsville
Virginia (16 letters)
5.= Chickasawhatchee
Georgia (16 letters)
5.= Eichelbergertown
Pennsylvania (16 letters)
5.= Nollidewabticook
Maine (16 letters)
9. Pongowayhaymock
Maine (15 letters)
10. Anasagunticook
Maine (14 letters)

The longest hyphenated names in the US are **Winchester-on-the-Severn**, Maryland, and **Washington-on-the-Brazos**, Texas, both of which contain 21 letters.

A number of long American place names are of Native American origin, but some are not as long as they once were: in 1916 the US Board on Geographic Names saw fit to reduce the 26-letter New Hampshire stream known as **Quohquinapassakessamanagno** to 'Beaver Creek', while the **Conamabsqunooncant** River became 'Duck'.

Short place names

One letter

A
A Danish village (spelled Å) on Fyn island

E
A river in Scotland

L
A lake in Nebraska, USA

T
A gulch in Colorado, USA

U
A place in the Caroline Islands

Y
A French village

There are many three-letter British place names, among them Nax, Bix, Cog, Wig, Ide, three Eyes (or rather, three places called Eye), Hey, Hoe, How, Hoy and Hoo, with Ham (17 examples) being the commonest.

Two letters

Ae
Dumfries and Galloway, Scotland

Bu
Place on Orkney

Ea
Inlet in Ireland

Ed
Kentucky, USA

Oa
Place on the island of Islay, Scotland

Or
Kentucky, USA

Oz
Kentucky, USA

Ta
Place name in Ireland

Uz
Kentucky, USA

Misleading Place Names

Boring, Oregon

Named after founder W. H. Boring.
Apparently it is not as dull as it sounds, since the
town's slogan is 'The most exciting place to live!'

CROWDS GATHER IN BORING TO WATCH THE ANNUAL 'CHANGING OF THE TRAFFIC LIGHT'

Buenos Aires, Argentina

The name of the capital of Argentina means 'good winds' – but not because the city is windy. Part of the original full name included 'Our Lady the Virgin Mary of Good Winds' – because sailors prayed to her to grant them favourable winds for their sailing ships.

Cape of Good Hope

The sea off south-west Africa was originally called *Cabo Tormentoso*, or 'Cape of Storms', by Portuguese sailor Bartolomeu Dias, who first sailed round it in 1488. The Portuguese king John II thought it an unpleasant name, and one that would deter future explorers, so he renamed it *Cabo da Boa Esperança*, or 'Cape of Good Hope'.

Greenland

Some 85% of Greenland is not green at all, but white, as the country is covered with ice. It is said that its name was invented in 982 by Norse sailor Erik the Red, who was hoping to encourage his countrymen to settle there.

Nome, Alaska
The Alaskan port was marked by a British map-maker as 'Name?' Unfortunately his handwriting was not very good, and so his scribbled question became the name of the city.

The Pacific Ocean
When he crossed it in 1520–21, the explorer Ferdinand Magellan named it *Mar Pacífico*, meaning calm sea. He was lucky, as what we now call the Pacific Ocean can experience some of the stormiest weather in the world, along with huge tsunamis (tidal waves).

Pago Pago, Samoa
It is said that the correct name of the port on the Pacific island of Samoa is 'Pango Pango', but 19th-century missionaries who were printing a newspaper there did not have not enough 'n's when they printed the heading, and so they left them off, changing it to Pago Pago.

Singapore
The name means 'City of Lions', but no lions have ever been seen there (so far as we know!).

Why, Arizona
Actually named after the Y-shaped intersection on which it was built.

Yucatán Peninsula, Mexico
According to one account, the Spanish explorer Francisco Hernández de Córdoba asked a local tribesman what he called the Mexican peninsula; the man replied *'Yukatán'*, which means 'I don't understand you'.

The Largest Cities Named After Real or Mythical People

1. New York, USA
Duke of York

2. São Paulo, Brazil
St Paul

3. Mumbai, India
Mumba (goddess)

4. Calcutta, India
Kali (goddess)

5. Dacca, Bangladesh
Durga (goddess)

6. Washington, USA
George Washington

7. Johannesburg, South Africa
Johannes Rissik

8. San Francisco, USA
St Francis

Cities That Changed Their Names

Many cities changed their names after gaining independence, throwing off ones that had been imposed by colonists, or following political changes, such as those ending the former Soviet Union. Some changes, such as Bombay to Mumbai, India, and Peking to Beijing, China, have resulted from alterations to the way in which foreign languages are transliterated (translated from one alphabet to another).

Batavia, Indonesia
Jakarta (1949)

Canton, China
Guangzhou (1949)

Christiania, Norway
Oslo (1924)

Ciudad Trujillo, Dominican Republic
Santo Domingo (1961)

Byzantium/Constantinople, Turkey
Istanbul (1930)

Danzig, Poland
Gdansk (1945)

Edo, Japan
Tokyo (1868)

Leningrad, USSR
St Petersburg, Russia (1991)

Léopoldville, Belgian Congo
Kinshasa, Zaire (1960)

Madras, India
Chennai (1996)

New Amsterdam, America
New York, USA (1664)

Rangoon, Burma
Yangon, Myanmar (1989)

Saigon, Vietnam
Ho Chi Minh City (1975)

Salisbury, Rhodesia
Harare, Zimbabwe (1980)

Santa Isabel, Equatorial Guinea
Malabo (1973)

Tsaritsyn/Stalingrad, USSR
Volgograd, Russia (1961)

City Nicknames

The Granite City Aberdeen
Named for the regional granite used in
many of the buildings there.

Athens of the North Edinburgh
It has been so-called since the 18th century, when,
like Athens, Greece, the city became famous for its
culture and elegant architecture.

The Bride of the Sea Venice, Italy
Traditionally, the Doge (ruler) of Venice sailed into the Adriatic on Ascension Day, dropping a wedding ring into the sea as a symbol of Venice's status as a sea power.

The City of David Jerusalem, Israel
It is called this in the Bible – a reference to King David.

The City of Light Paris, France
The city is notable for its colourful nightlife.

The City of Dreaming Spires Oxford
Coined by the poet Matthew Arnold.

The Eternal City Rome, Italy
This nickname was first used by classical writers to describe the enduring quality of the city's great architecture.

The Big Apple New York, USA
The nickname has been used since the 1960s, but it was used earlier to describe New Orleans. It comes from a translation of *manzana principal*, Spanish for the main apple orchard, or most important place.

The Smoke London
Until recent times, thousands of chimneys in homes and factories belched out so much soot and smoke that London was often shrouded in thick fog.

Venice of the North Amsterdam, The Netherlands
The city's many canals and bridges led to this comparison with Venice, Italy – though Stockholm, Sweden, is also sometimes called the Venice of the North.

The Windy City Chicago, USA

Being built beside a large lake, Chicago is not only truly windy, but when it announced it wished to stage the Columbian Exposition in 1893, *New York Sun* editor Charles A. Dana called it that 'windy' city because of its presumptuousness.

Motown Detroit, USA

A shortening of 'Motor Town', from the days when this city was a centre of car manufacturing.

What Do You Call a Person from . . . ?

If people from London are Londoners and people from New York are New Yorkers, then shouldn't people from Manchester be . . . *Manchesterers*? Sadly, the names of inhabitants of cities are not usually that simple! Here are some of the trickier ones:

Aberdonian
Aberdeen

Angeleno
Los Angeles, USA

Bruxellois
Brussels, Belgium

Buffalonian
Buffalo, USA

Calcuttan
Calcutta, India

Cantabrigian
Cambridge

Cestrian
Chester

Chicagoan
Chicago, USA

Dallasite
Dallas, USA

Dubliner
Dublin

Dundonian
Dundee

Dunelmian
Durham (city)

Glaswegian
Glasgow

Hagenaar
The Hague, the Netherlands

Hamburger
Hamburg, Germany

Liverpudlian
Liverpool

Mancunian
Manchester

Muscovite
Moscow, Russia

Osloer
Oslo, Norway

Oxonian
Oxford

Parisian (man)/Parisienne (woman)
Paris, France

Pomponian
Portsmouth

Salopian
Shropshire

Tangerine
Tangier, Morocco

Trojan
Troy, USA

Yucatec
Yucatán, Mexico

Zürcher
Zurich, Switzerland

Fictitious British Towns and Villages

Abbot's Cernel
From Thomas Hardy's *Tess of the D'Urbervilles*

Ambridge
Setting for the radio series *The Archers*

Balamory
A Scottish island in the children's TV series

Blackbury
A town in Terry Pratchett's *Bromeliad* and Johnny Maxwell books

Brigadoon
A magical Scottish village from a musical of the same name

Camberwick Green
A village in a 1960s children's TV series

Crampton Hodnet
A comic novel by Barbara Pym

Crinkley Bottom
From *Noel's House Party*, a 1990s light-entertainment show

Dibley
From *The Vicar of Dibley*, a TV comedy series

East Bromwich
From the *Hellboy* comics

Elsinby
From the medical drama *The Royal*

Emmerdale
From the soap opera of the same name

Greendale
Village in the *Postman Pat* children's series

Harchester
From *Dream Team*, football-based soap opera

Holby
Setting for *Casualty*, a medical drama

Lambton
From Jane Austen's *Pride and Prejudice*

Leadworth
Home town of Amy Pond in the 2010 series of *Doctor Who*

Little Whinging
Harry Potter's home town in the novels by J.K. Rowling

Middlemarch
From the novel by George Eliot

Nutwood
From the *Rupert the Bear* books

Ottery St Catchpole
A village in the *Harry Potter* books

Pontypandy
From *Fireman Sam*, the children's series

Royston Vasey
Setting for *The League of Gentlemen*, comedy series

Rummidge
Used by David Lodge in many of his novels

Skelthwaite
From the television drama *Where the Heart Is*

St Mary Mead
Home of Miss Marple in Agatha Christie's stories

Tidmouth
The largest town on the Island of Sodor in
Thomas the Tank Engine

Totleigh-in-the-Wold
Village in P. G. Wodehouse's *Jeeves and Wooster* stories

Trumpton
From the children's TV series of the same name

Walford
From the soap opera *EastEnders*

Walmington-on-Sea
Setting for *Dad's Army*, the TV comedy series

Weatherfield
Setting for the soap opera *Coronation Street*

4. STREETS AND HOUSES

Top Street Names in the UK

1. High Street
2. Station Road
3. Main Street
4. Park Road
5. Church Road
6. Church Street
7. London Road
8. Victoria Road
9. Green Lane
10. Manor Road
11. Church Lane
12. Park Avenue
13. The Avenue
14. The Crescent
15. Queens Road
16. New Road
17. Grange Road
18. Kings Road
19. Kingsway
20. Windsor Road

Top Street Names in the USA

Most towns and cities in Great Britain have grown and evolved over centuries, but as America is a relatively new country, many of its towns were carefully planned by settlers as grids of streets running from north to south, crossed with streets running from east to west. These streets are often numbered in order rather than given individual names, which is why there are so many numbers on this list.

1. Second	11. Pine
2. Third	12. Maple
3. First	13. Cedar
4. Fourth	14. Eighth
5. Park	15. Elm
6. Fifth	16. View
7. Main	17. Washington
8. Sixth	18. Ninth
9. Oak	19. Lake
10. Seventh	20. Hill

Surprisingly, 'First' is not first in the list, as many streets that would be so designated are called Main Street instead. Washington is the highest-ranked street name derived from a personal name.

Unusual Street Names in the UK

Bag Lane
Ballybogey Road
Balruddery Place
Bedlam Street
Beggars Bush Lane
Blinkbonny Road
Bordom Hill
Bottom Street
Bright Green Street
Burniebuzzle Crescent

Butt Lane
Buzzacott Lane
Cackle Street
Cake Street
Crazy Lane
Creampot Close
Dumber Lane
Elf Row
Eureka Road
Fartown
Fishey Lane
Flapper Fold Lane
Foggyley Gardens
Football
Frying Pan Alley
Gillygooley Road
Goosedubs Street
Happy Land
Happyhillock Road
Hearts Delight Road
Holy Bones
Itchin Close
Jammy Lane
Jaunty Way
Land of Green Ginger
Little Shambles

Loonies Court
Lower Back of the Walls
Mudlarks Way
Mullaghnamoyagh Road
Mullydoo Road
My Lord's Road
Nameplate Close
Needless Road
No Name Street
Nutter Street
Pant-y-Pistyll
Pickles Lane
Pie Corner
The Pigs Walk

Ponker Nook Lane
Poppit Street
Porridge Pot Alley
Potto Street
Quaggy Walk
Randiddles Close
Ribadoo Road
Rotten Row
Scratchface Lane
Scumbrum Lane
Silly Lane
Smellies Lane
Snail Creep Lane
Squeeze Guts Alley
Tarmac Road
There and Back Again Lane
Tickle Avenue
Tongue Lane
Trash Lane
Warning Tongue Lane
Wash Lane
Whip-Ma-Wop-Ma Gate
Zed Alley
Zin Zan Street

Unusual Street Names in London

Birdcage Walk
Bird-in-Bush Road
Bleeding Heart Yard
Bullocks Terrace
Crooked Usage
Crutched Friars
Friday Street
Garlic Hill
Ha-Ha Road
Hanging Sword Alley
Honeypot Lane
Mincing Land
Petty France
Pope's Head Alley
Shoulder of Mutton Alley
Threadneedle Street
Throgmorton Street
Seething Lane
Shower Curtain Street
Wardrobe Terrace

Top House Names in the UK

1. The Cottage
2. Rose Cottage

3. The Bungalow
4. The Coach House
5. Orchard House
6. The Lodge
7. Woodlands
8. The Old School House
9. Ivy Cottage
10. The Willows
11. The Barn
12. The Old Rectory
13. Hillside
14. Hillcrest
15. The Croft
16. The Old Vicarage
17. Sunnyside
18. Orchard Cottage
19. Yew Tree Cottage
20. The Laurels

Part 2:

Botty

PEOPLE

1. FIRST NAMES FIRST

The Most Unusual First Names

Strange but true – every one of these first names was given to at least one person in the past!

Abba	Baboon	Blood	Chimp	Dolphin
Absolutely	Bacardi	Blotter	Chocolate	Dumbo
Absurd	Bad	Bogey	Choochoo	Duvet
Adder	Badger	Bomb	Christmas	Dynamite
Agony	Baldy	Bottle	Chutney	Earless
Ah	Banana	Botty	Cod	Earthquake
Albatross	Banger	Bounce	Cool	Eel
Alien	Bash	Bovril	Crash	Eggy
Angry	Bat	Brains	Crazy	Elastic
Argos	Beatles	Bubble	Creature	Electric
Armadillo	Belch	Burp	Cricket	Elephant
Arrow	Bendy	Butter	Cuckoo	Emperor
Arsenal	Billion	Cabbage	Cupboard	Emu
Aspirin	Birdseye	Camel	Custard	Encyclo-pedia Britannica
Atomic	Birming-ham	Carpet	Daft	
Audi	Biscuit	Cash	Dangerous	Enormous
Auk	Blackberry	Cement	Dim	Evil
Avatar		Cheese	Dirty	Excellent
Awful	Blender	Chicken	Doctor	

Exmeater	Hamster	Mole	Pudding	Toffee
Fairy	Handy	Monster	Quack	Toilet
Famous	Hippo	Muck	Quasimodo	Tomato
Fang	Hitler	Muffin	Rhubarb	Tornado
Farty	Hobbit	Muppet	Salami	Trainers
Fat	Honk	Murder	Sandwich	Treacle
Fatty	Hopeless	Mustard	Sardine	Trouser
Filthy	Horrible	Nasty	Scary	Turkey
Fish	Idiot	Nutella	Sick	Ugly
Floppy	Ipad	Nylon	Skeleton	University
Forget	Jam	Odd	Sloth	Uranus
Freak	Jedward	Ordeal	Sludge	Uzzle
Fridge	Jelly	Ostrich	Snowman	Vanilla
Frightful	Kangaroo	Otter	Soggy	Vermin
Gaga	Landrover	Oxygen	Spider	Volcano
Geek	Lasagna	Oyster	Submarine	Walnut
Ginger	Lemonade	Pants	Swine	Wardrobe
Giraffe	Limousine	Peculiar	Teapot	Watercress
Gnome	Lizard	Pickles	Telegraph	Weedy
Goat	Lollipop	Pig	Tesco	Whale-belly
Goblin	Mad	Pirate	Thick	Zebra
Gorilla	Magnet	Poo	Thirteen	Zip
Grasshopper	Malaria	Preserved	Thirty	Zonk
Gravy	Marmalade	President	Thousand	Zoom
Hairy	Marmite	Pringles	Three	
Halloween	Million	Professor	Toast	

Top First Names in England and Wales

(figures taken from 2009)

See if your name is in one of these lists . . .

Girls

1. Olivia

Adapted from the male name Oliver, first used by
Shakespeare in his play, *Twelfth Night* (1599).

2. Ruby

From the Latin word for 'red', and the gemstone. A fashionable
19th-century name, it has had a comeback in recent years.

3. Chloe

From a Greek word meaning 'young green shoot', one of the
many names of Demeter, goddess of the harvest.

4. Emily

From the Latin name Aemilia.

5. Sophie

From the Greek, meaning 'wisdom'.
Popular since the 18th century.

6. Jessica

Jessica in Shakespeare's play *The Merchant of Venice* (1596)
brought this name to public attention.

7. Grace

From the Latin for 'thanks'. The name was popular in the

19th century when Grace Darling, who rescued shipwrecked sailors, was a national heroine, and again in the 20th century when actress Grace Kelly became Princess Grace of Monaco.

8. Lily

From the lily flower, a symbol of purity.

9. Amelia

Like Emily, from the Latin. It was first used as the title of a book by Henry Fielding in 1751. More recently, *Doctor Who* has featured the character Amelia Pond.

10. Evie

From Eve, the very first woman (according to the Bible). It comes from the Hebrew word for life.

11. Mia

A Scandinavian version of Maria, it became popular after the success of actress Mia Farrow.

12. Ava

Of uncertain origin; possibly German, or from the Latin word for bird, 'avis'. It has grown in popularity since the success of American movie actress Ava Gardner in the 1950s.

13. Ella

A version of Ellen, it came to England with the Normans.

14. Charlotte

The female version of Charles, it became popular in the 18th and 19th centuries after Queen Charlotte and the novelist Charlotte Brontë.

15. Isabella

A variant of Isabelle and Elizabeth, meaning 'God's promise'.

16. Lucy

From the Latin for light, and the male name Lucius.

17. Isabelle

See 'Isabella' (15).

18. Daisy

The name of the flower actually comes from an
old English word meaning 'day's eye'.

19. Holly

The tree's name comes from the old English word 'holegn'.

20. Megan

Originally a shortened, pet name for Margaret.

Boys

1. Oliver

A Latin word, possibly from the olive plant, or
from the German name Olaf.

2. Jack

A version of John, from the Hebrew 'gracious gift of God'.

3. Harry

In medieval England, this was the spoken version of Henry,
and both names come from the Germanic name Haimirich,
which means 'home ruler'.

4. Alfie

A shortened version of Alfred, which means 'elf council'.

5. Joshua

From the Hebrew word 'Yenoshua' – 'God is salvation'.

6. Thomas

From the Aramaic language – 'a twin'.

7. Charlie

A shortening of Charles, from the Germanic
word for 'a free man'.

8. William

From the Germanic words for 'resolution' and 'helmet'.

9. James

Of Hebrew origin, meaning 'may God protect' or 'supplanter'.

10. Daniel

Of Hebrew origin, meaning 'judged of God'.

11. George

Of ancient Greek origin; 'earth-worker' or 'farmer'.

12. Samuel

Of Hebrew origin; 'His name is God' or 'God hath heard'.

13. Ethan

Of Hebrew origin, meaning 'firmness', 'long-lived'.

14. Joseph

Of Hebrew origin – 'may God add'.

15. Benjamin

Of Hebrew origin – 'son of my right hand', 'son of the south'.

16. Mohammed

Of Arabic origin, meaning 'praiseworthy'. The name of the Prophet and founder of Islam.

17. Lucas

A variant of Luke, it refers to someone who is 'from Lucanas', a place in southern Italy.

18. Jacob

Has the same meaning as James (9).

19. Dylan

Of Welsh origin – 'son of the sea'.

20. Archie

A shortened version of Archibald, which means 'genuine', 'bold', 'brave'.

Top First Names in Scotland

(figures taken from 2009)

Girls	Boys
1. Sophie	1. Jack
2. Olivia	2. Lewis
3. Ava	3. James
4. Emily	4. Liam
5. Lucy	5. Logan
6. Chloe	6. Daniel
7. Katie	7. Aaron
8. Emma	8. Ryan
9. Amy	9. Cameron
10. Erin	10. Callum
11. Isla	11. Alexander
12. Ellie	12. Finlay
13. Jessica	13. Jamie
14. Hannah	14. Aiden
15. Grace	15. Dylan
16. Lily	16. Lucas
17. Eva	17.= Kyle
18. Brooke	17.= Matthew
19. Leah	19. Adam
20. Mia	20. Nathan

Top First Names in Northern Ireland

(figures taken from 2009)

Girls	Boys
1. Katie	1. Jack
2. Sophie	2. Matthew
3. Grace	3.= Daniel
4. Lucy	3.= James
5. Erin	5. Ryan
6. Emily	6. Adam
7. Emma	7. Ethan
8. Eva	8. Charlie
9. Chloe	9. Thomas
10. Anna	10. Conor
11. Jessica	11.= Dylan
12. Hannah	11.= Jamie
13.= Aoife	13. Harry
13.= Ellie	14. Aaron
15. Amy	15. Callum
16. Sarah	16. Joshua
17. Olivia	17. Oliver
18. Niamh	18. Sean
19. Ella	19. Ben
20. Aimee	20.= Jake
	20.= Luke

First Names Through History

Lists of popular names are always changing as different ones fall in and out of fashion. Here are some of the most popular names from different periods of British history.

Top Names in Medieval England

These are the most common names found in documents from the late 12th to late 13th centuries.

Girls	Boys
1. Alice	1. William
2. Matilda	2. John
3. Joan	3. Robert
4. Agnes	4. Richard
5. Emma	5. Roger
6. Isabela/ Isabella	6. Ralph
7. Margery	7. Thomas
8. Cristiana/ Christiania	8. Henry
9. Roesia/ Rohesia	9. Geoffrey
10. Juliana	10. Walter

Top Names in Elizabethan England

These are the most popular names of boys and girls of the late 16th century. As Shakespeare would have been familiar with these, many of them are the names of characters in his plays. Queen Elizabeth I was on the throne at this time, so it is not surprising that her name is at the top of the girls' list.

Girls

1. Elizabeth
2. Anne
3. Joan
4. Margaret
5. Alice
6. Mary
7. Agnes
8. Catherine
9. Jane
10. Dorothy

Boys

1. John
2. Thomas
3. William
4. Richard
5. Robert
6. Henry
7. George
8. Edward
9. Nicholas
10. James

Top Names in the 1700s

Queen Elizabeth I died in 1603, but the name remained very popular for quite a while. Watch how it slips down the rankings over the next few hundred years . . .

Girls	Boys
1. Mary	1. John
2. Elizabeth	2. William
3. Ann	3. Thomas
4. Sarah	4. Richard
5. Jane	5. James
6. Margaret	6. Robert
7. Susan	7. Joseph
8. Martha	8. Edward
9. Hannah	9. Henry
10. Catherine	10. George

Top Names in the 1800s

Girls	Boys
1. Mary	1. William
2. Ann	2. John
3. Elizabeth	3. Thomas
4. Sarah	4. James
5. Jane	5. George
6. Hannah	6. Joseph
7. Susan	7. Richard
8. Martha	8. Henry
9. Margaret	9. Robert
10. Charlotte	10. Charles

Top Names in the 1900s

Girls

1. Mary
2. Florence
3. Doris
4. Edith
5. Dorothy
6. Annie
7. Margaret
8. Alice
9. Elizabeth
10. Elsie

Boys

1. William
2. John
3. George
4. Thomas
5. Arthur
6. James
7. Charles
8. Frederick
9. Albert
10. Ernest

Top Names in the 1950s

As we approach our own era, we can see how much names have changed – seven of the boys' names on this list didn't feature in any of our other historical top tens.

Girls

1. Susan
2. Linda
3. Christine
4. Margaret
5. Janet
6. Patricia
7. Carol
8. Elizabeth
9. Mary
10. Anne

Boys

1. David	6. Robert
2. John	7. Paul
3. Stephen	8. Alan
4. Michael	9. Christopher
5. Peter	10. Richard

Top Names in the 1990s

Girls

1. Rebecca
2. Lauren
3. Jessica
4. Charlotte
5. Hannah
6. Sophie
7. Amy
8. Emily
9. Laura
10. Emma

Boys

1. Thomas
2. James
3. Jack
4. Daniel
5. Matthew
6. Ryan
7. Joshua
8. Luke
9. Samuel
10. Jordan

Top Names in the 2000s

Girls

1. Emily
2. Ellie
3. Jessica
4. Sophie
5. Chloe
6. Lucy
7. Olivia
8. Charlotte
9. Katie
10. Megan

Boys

1. Jack
2. Joshua
3. Thomas
4. James
5. Daniel
6. Samuel
7. Oliver
8. William
9. Benjamin
10. Joseph

The Most Common First Names Ever in England & Wales

(based on births registered 1837–2005)

As you can see from the lists above, some names fall in and out of fashion, but some remain consistently popular. Here are the most popular names in the UK over the past two centuries.

Girls

Mary
Elizabeth
Ann
Jane
Sarah
Margaret
Alice
Ellen
Annie

Boys

John
William
James
Thomas
George
Henry
David
Charles
Robert

First Names from the USA

Including American names in *Boring, Botty and Spong* doesn't mean that they are in any way stranger than British names (although some of them are!). The United States has often been called a 'melting pot' of immigrants, with a variety of people – and names – that come from different cultures.

Top First Names in the USA

(figures taken from 2009)

Girls

1. Isabella
2. Emma
3. Olivia
4. Sophia
5. Ava
6. Emily
7. Madison
8. Abigail
9. Chloe
10. Mia
11. Elizabeth
12. Addison
13. Alexis
14. Ella
15. Samantha
16. Natalie
17. Grace
18. Lily
19. Alyssa
20. Ashley

Boys

1. Jacob	11. Christopher
2. Ethan	12. Aiden
3. Michael	13. Matthew
4. Alexander	14. David
5. William	15. Andrew
6. Joshua	16. Joseph
7. Daniel	17. Logan
8. Jayden	18. James
9. Noah	19. Ryan
10. Anthony	20. Benjamin

Some people have claimed that Jacob and Isabella are America's most popular first names because of Jacob Black and Isabella Swann, two of the main characters in Stephanie Meyer's *Twilight* book and film series. However, Jacob has been at number one since 1999 and Isabella had already risen to number six when the first book was published in 2005. On the other hand, Bella, as Isabella is known in the series, has steadily gone up in recent years – the name was not even in the top 1,000 in 1999, but reached 58 in 2009.

Top First Names of the 1900s in the USA

Girls

1. Mary
2. Helen
3. Margaret
4. Anna
5. Ruth
6. Elizabeth
7. Dorothy
8. Marie
9. Florence
10. Mildred

Boys

1. John
2. William
3. James
4. George
5. Charles
6. Robert
7. Joseph
8. Frank
9. Edward
10. Thomas

Top First Names of the 1950s in the USA

Girls

1. Mary
2. Linda
3. Patricia
4. Susan
5. Deborah

6. Barbara
7. Debra
8. Karen
9. Nancy
10. Donna

Boys

1. James	6. William
2. Michael	7. Richard
3. Robert	8. Thomas
4. John	9. Mark
5. David	10. Charles

Top First Names of the 1990s in the USA

Girls

1. Jessica
2. Ashley
3. Emily
4. Sarah
5. Samantha
6. Amanda
7. Brittany
8. Elizabeth
9. Taylor
10. Megan

Boys

1. Michael
2. Christopher
3. Matthew
4. Joshua
5. Jacob
6. Nicholas
7. Andrew
8. Daniel
9. Tyler
10. Joseph

Top First Names of the 2000s in the USA

Girls	Boys
1. Emily	1. Jacob
2. Madison	2. Michael
3. Emma	3. Joshua
4. Olivia	4. Matthew
5. Hannah	5. Daniel
6. Abigail	6. Christopher
7. Isabella	7. Andrew
8. Samantha	8. Ethan
9. Elizabeth	9. Joseph
10. Ashley	10. William

Top First Names of Twins Born in the USA, 2009

Female Twins

1. Isabella and Sophia
2. Faith and Hope
3.= Olivia and Sophia
3.= Ella and Emma
5. Hailey and Hannah

Male Twins

1. Jacob and Joshua
2. Matthew and Michael
3. Daniel and David
4. Jayden and Jordan
5. Jayden and Jaylen

Male and Female Twins

1. Madison and Michael
2. Taylor and Tyler
3. Addison and Aiden
4.= Emily and Ethan
4.= Emma and Evan

....

The Most Common First Names Ever in the USA

(based on births registered 1880–2009)

Girls

Mary	Jennifer
Patricia	Maria
Linda	Susan
Barbara	Margaret
Elizabeth	Dorothy

Boys

James	David
John	Richard
Robert	Charles
Michael	Joseph
William	Thomas

....

Coast to Coast

The Top First Names in California and New York, 2009

The USA is so big compared to the UK that it's interesting to see how different names are on one side of the country from the other . . .

California
Girls

1. Isabella	6. Natalie
2. Sophia	7. Emma
3. Emily	8. Ashley
4. Mia	9. Abigail
5. Samantha	10. Olivia

Boys

1. Daniel	6. Ethan
2. Anthony	7. David
3. Angel	8. Andrew
4. Jacob	9. Matthew
5. Alexander	10. Joshua

New York

Girls

Boys

Girls	Boys
1. Isabella	1. Michael
2. Sophia	2. Jayden
3. Olivia	3. Matthew
4. Emma	4. Ethan
5. Emily	5. Daniel
6. Madison	6. Ryan
7. Ava	7. Anthony
8. Mia	8. Joseph
9. Abigail	9. Jacob
10. Sarah	10. Christopher

The 10 Least Popular First Names in the USA, 1880s

There may be good reasons why rare names are rare, and for American parents the US Social Security Administration helpfully indicates these by publishing surveys of the most and least popular first names in the United States – the least being those that feature at the bottom of a table of the top 1,000. For example, while in the 1880s 91,673 girls were called Mary, a mere 39 received the name Eura . . .

Girls

1. Eura
2. Missie
3. Biddie
4. Mannie
5. Libby
6. Johannah
7. Leana
8. Media
9. Hertha
10. Reta

Boys

1. Ammon
2. Ewald
3. Brice
4. Linton
5. Vester
6. Reinhold
7. Ewing
8. Stanton
9. Moody
10. Kelley

The 10 Least Popular First Names in the USA, 2000s

Girls

1. Jacklyn
2. Kimora
3. Allyssa
4. Jeanette
5. Chandler
6. Phoenix
7. Mina
8. Sheridan
9. Kristine
10. Sarina

Boys

1. Terence
2. Lonnie
3. Kelly
4. Maximo
5. Garett
6. Devante
7. Mitchel
8. Joan
9. Soren
10. Matthias

First Names from Around the World

Now let's take a look at recent lists of the most
popular names from some other countries

Australia

(based on registrations in New South Wales)

Girls	Boys
1. Isabella	1. William
2. Chloe	2. Jack
3. Charlotte	3. Lachlan
4. Olivia	4. Cooper
5. Mia	5. Joshua
6. Emily	6. Thomas
7.= Sophie	7. Oliver
7.= Ella	8. Noah
9. Sienna	9. Ethan
10. Amelia	10. Riley

France
Girls

1. Emma	6. Lea
2. Clara	7. Chloe
3. Manon	8. Ines
4. Camille	9. Sarah
5. Jade	10. Lola

Boys

1. Enzo	6. Lucas
2. Nathan	7. Mathis
3. Louis	8. Thomas
4. Hugo	9. Theo
5. Raphael	10. Matheo

Germany

Girls

1. Marie
2. Sophie/Sofie
3. Maria
4. Anna
5. Emma
6. Mia
7. Sophia/Sofia
8. Leonie
9. Lena
10. Johanna

Boys

1. Maximilian
2. Alexander
3. Leon
4. Paul
5. Luca/Luka
6. Elias
7. Felix
8. Lukas/Lucas
9. Jonas
10. David

Ireland

Girls

1. Ava
2. Katie
3. Sarah
4. Emma
5. Emily
6. Sophie
7. Grace
8. Aiofe
9. Chloe
10. Kate

Boys

1. Jack
2. Sean
3. Conor
4. Daniel
5. James
6. Ryan
7. Adam
8. Dylan
9. Luke
10. Alex

The Netherlands

Girls

1. Emma
2. Julia
3. Lotte
4. Sophie
5. Lisa
6. Lieke
7. Noa
8. Fleur
9. Anna
10. Tess

Boys

1. Lucas
2. Sem
3. Tim
4. Thomas
5. Stijn
6. Daan
7. Thijs
8. Milan
9. Reuben
10. Jesse

Norway

Girls

1. Emma
2. Linnea/Linea
3. Nora/Norah
4. Sofie/Sophie
5. Sara/Sahra/
   Sarah
6. Thea/Tea
7. Emilie
8. Ida
9.= Ingrid/
   Ingerid/Ingri
9.= Julie

Boys

1. Lucas/Lukas
2. Emil
3. Alexander/
   Aleksander
4. Oliver
5. Mathias/
   Matias
6. Jonas
7. Markus/
   Marcus
8. William
9.= Magnus
9.= Sande

Spain

(these are the most popular names of people
alive in Spain rather than births)

Girls

1. María
2. Carmen
3. María Del Carmen
4. Josefa
5. Isabel

6. Dolores
7. Francisca
8. Antonia
9. Pilar
10. María Dolores

Boys

1. José	6. Pedro
2. Antonio	7. José Luis
3. Manuel	8. Jesús
4. Francisco	9. Ángel
5. Juan	10. Luis

Sweden

Girls

Boys

Girls	Boys
1. Maria	1. Erik
2. Elisabeth	2. Karl
3. Anna	3. Lars
4. Kristina	4. Anders
5. Margareta	5. Per
6. Eva	6. Johan
7. Birgitta	7. Mikael
8. Karin	8. Olof
9. Linnéa	9. Nils
10. Marie	10. Lennart

First Names Invented by Writers

Some names that are popular today, or have been used in the past, were invented by or first used by writers as character names in their novels or plays. Some, such as Wendy, may already have been used occasionally, but when the books in which they appeared became popular, many parents chose the names for their children.

Adriana
William Shakespeare, *The Comedy of Errors* (1592)

Araminta
Sir John Vanbrugh, *The Confederacy* (1695)

Belinda
Henry Purcell and Nahum Tate, *Dido and Aeneas* (1689)

Berinthia
Colley Cibber, *Love's Last Shift* (1696)

Dorian
Oscar Wilde, *The Picture of Dorian Gray* (1890)

Dorinda
George Farquhar, *The Beaux' Stratagem* (1707)

Evangeline
Henry Wadsworth Longfellow, *Evangeline* (1847)

Gloria
Emma Southworth, *Gloria* (1891)

Haidee
Lord Byron, *Don Juan* (1819–24)

Janice
Paul Leicester Ford, *Janice Meredith* (1899)

Jessica
William Shakespeare, *The Merchant of Venice* (1596)

Lucinda
Miguel Cervantes, *Don Quixote* (1610)

Malvina
James MacPherson, *Ossian* (1765)

Miranda
William Shakespeare, *The Tempest* (1610)

Olivia
William Shakespeare, *Twelfth Night* (1599)

Orville
Fanny Burney, *Evelina* (1778)

Pamela
Sir Philip Sidney, *Arcadia* (1590)

Perdita
William Shakespeare, *The Winter's Tale* (1610)

Regan
William Shakespeare, *King Lear* (1605)

Stella
Sir Philip Sidney, *Astrophel and Stella* (1591)

Thelma
Marie Corelli, *Thelma* (1886)

Vanessa

Jonathan Swift, *Cadenus and Vanessa* (1726)

Viola

William Shakespeare, *Twelfth Night* (1599)

Wendy

J. M. Barry, *Peter Pan* (1904)

Zoraida

Miguel Cervantes, *Don Quixote* (1610)

Teachers' Pests

Britain's Naughtiest Kids' Names

It isn't just Santa Claus who makes lists of naughty children!
According to a poll of 3,000 teachers, the following names
are ones that they expect to cause trouble in class based upon
their past experiences with children of the same name.
Of course, just because teachers expect children to act
naughtily does not necessarily mean that they are naughty, so
if you have one of these names you might want to
behave extremely well to prove them wrong.

Girls

1. Chelsea
2. Courtney
3. Chardonnay
4. Aleisha
5. Casey

6. Crystal
7. Jessica
8. Brooke
9. Demi
10. Aisha

Boys

1. Callum	6. Charlie
2. Connor	7. Kyle
3. Jack	8. Liam
4. Daniel	9. Jake
5. Brandon	10. Brooklyn

. . . .

Top 10 'Criminal' Boys' Names in the USA

(listed alphabetically)

Recent research conducted by Professor David Kalist of Shippensburg University, Pennsylvania, published in *Social Science Quarterly* appears to indicate that certain first names, based on a study of more than 15,000, predispose their bearers to lead lives of crime. Whether this results from a bias against certain names, so that those who bear them are subjected to bullying and turn to crime remains unproven.

Alec	Luke
Ernest	Malcolm
Garland	Preston
Ivan	Tyrell
Kareem	Walter

Celebrity Baby Names

As we have seen, amusing names are by no means exclusive to famous people – but when celebrities do give their children unusual names it certainly does get talked about. Here is a selection of the more interesting baby names chosen by celebrities.

Amber Rose & Saffron Sahara
Simon Le Bon (musician) & Yasmin Le Bon (fashion model)

Apple
Chris Martin (musician) & Gwyneth Paltrow (actress)

Aurelius Cy
Elle Macpherson (fashion model) & Arpad Busson

Bluebell Madonna
Geri Halliwell (pop singer)

Brooklyn, Cruz, Romeo & Harper Seven
David Beckham (footballer) & Victoria Beckham (pop singer)

Chastity
Cher (singer) & Sonny Bono (musician)

Coco Lux
Jo Whiley (DJ) & Steve Morton

Daisy Boo, Petal Blossom Rainbow, Poppy Honey & Buddy Bear
Jamie Oliver (chef) & Jules Oliver

Denim Cole & Diezel Ky
Toni Braxton (musician) & Keri Lewis (musician)

Destry
Steven Spielberg (film director) & Kate Capshaw (actress)

Elijah Blue
Cher (singer) & Greg Allman (musician)

Ella Blue
John Travolta (actor) & Kelly Preston (actress)

Eric Mustard, Neil Marmalade & Vincent Mash
Helen Baxendale (actress) & David Williams (film director)

Fifi Trixibelle, Peaches Honeyblossom & Pixie

Bob Geldof (musician and activist) & Paula Yates (presenter)

Fuchsia

Sting (musician) & Frances Tomelty (actress)

Gaia

Emma Thompson (actress) & Greg Wise (actor)

God'Iss Love Stone & Heaven Love'on Stone

Lil' Mo (musician) & Al Stone

Harlow Winter Kate & Sparrow James Midnight

Nicole Richie (fashion designer) & Joel Madden (singer)

Heavenly Hiraani Tiger Lily

Michael Hutchence (musician) & Paula Yates (presenter)

Homer

Matt Groening (cartoonist) & Deborah Groening

Hopper

Sean Penn (actor) & Robin Wright (actress)

Ireland

Alec Baldwin (actor) & Kim Basinger (actress)

Jaden Gil & Jaz

Steffi Graf (tennis champion) & Andre Agassi (tennis champion)

Jermajesty
Jermaine Jackson (singer) & Alejandra Genevieve Oaziaza

Kal-El Coppola
Nicholas Cage (actor) & Alice Cage

Kyd
David Duchovny (actor) & Tea Leoni (actress)

Lark Song
Mia Farrow (actress) & André Previn (musician)

Lennon
Liam Gallagher (musician) & Patsy Kensit (actress)

Liberty Beau
Ryan Giggs (footballer) & Stacey Cooke

London Emilio & Cash Anthony
Slash (musician) & Perla Ferrar

Memphis Eve
Bono (musician) & Alison Hewson (activist)

Moon Unit
Frank Zappa (musician) & Adelaide Zappa

Moxie CrimeFighter & Zolten
Penn Jillette (magician) & Emily Jillette

Phoenix Chi
Mel B (singer) & Jimmy Gulzar

Pilot Inspektor
Jason Lee (actor) & Beth Riesgraf (actress)

Piper Maru
Gillian Anderson (actress) & Clyde Klotz

Prince Michael I & Prince Michael II (nicknamed 'Blanket')
Michael Jackson (musician)

Princess Tiaamii
Katie Price (model) & Peter Andre (musician)

Racer Maximilliano, Rebel Antonio, Rocket Valentino & Rogue Joaquin
Robert Rodriguez (film director)
& Elizabeth Rodriguez (film producer)

Rumer Glenn, Scout LaRue & Tallulah Belle
Bruce Willis (actor) & Demi Moore (actress)

Sage Moonblood & Seargeoh
Sylvester Stallone (actor) & Sasha Czack

Sam Bazooka
Elliot Gould (actor) & Jennifer Gould

Satchel
Woody Allen (film director) & Mia Farrow (actress)

Sonnet & True
Forest Whitaker (actor) & Keisha Whitaker

Speck Wildhorse
John Cougar Mellencamp (musician)
& Elaine Irwin Mellencamp (supermodel)

Sunday Rose

Nicole Kidman (actress) & Keith Urban (musician)

Tara Gabriel Galaxy Gramophone

Sir John Paul Getty (philanthropist) & Talitha Getty (model)

Zola Ivy

Eddie Murphy (actor) & Nicole Mitchell

Zowie

David Bowie (musician) & Angela Bowie

Zuma Nesta Rock

Gwen Stefani (musician) & Gavin Rossdale (musician)

Named After a Celebrity?

A 2006 survey of birth certificates since 1984 revealed that there are a lot of children in the country who share their names with celebrities. Of course, we can't be certain in every case that the names were picked because of the famous person, but it certainly must have influenced some of them.

Girls

Kiera (8,716)	**Peaches (472)**
Kylie (7,216)	**Madonna (288)**
Shakira (2,614)	**Dido (48)**
Britney (1,611)	**Apple (2)**

Boys

Tiger (1,191)	Jay-Z (7)
Keanu (1,120)	Gandalf (6)
Dre (426)	Snoop (3)
Gazza (39)	David Beckham (3)
Brooklyn (28)	Superman (2)
Tupac (27)	

Male to Female Names

Many first names that started off as male have been turned into female ones over time. Often this was because parents wanted to use the name of a grandfather or other male member of the family, but as they did not have a son, gave the female version to their daughter. Here are some examples:

Adrian	Adriana
Alan	Alana
Albert	Alberta
Alexander	Alexandra
Andrew	Andrea
Anthony	Antonia
Daniel	Danielle
Denis	Denise
Dominic	Dominique
Edwin	Edwina

Eric	Erica
Gabriel	Gabrielle
Geralde	Geraldine
George	Georgia
Harry	Harriet
Henry	Henrietta
Josephe	Josephine
Kyle	Kylie
Louis	Louisa
Marcus	Marcia
Martin	Martine
Max	Maxine
Michael	Michelle
Nigel	Nigella
Norman	Norma
Octavius	Octavia
Patrick	Patricia
Paul	Paula
Philip	Philippa
Robert	Roberta
Stephen	Stephanie

Jewel Names for Girls

Lots of girls take their first names
from jewels or precious stones.

Amber
Amethyst
Aqua(marine)
Beryl
Coral
Crystal
Diamond
Esmeralda (Emerald)
Garnet
Gemma (Jemma)
Jade (Jada)
Jet, Jetta
Jewel
Onyx
Opal
Pearl
Ruby

2. THE LAST WORD ON LAST NAMES – SURNAMES

● ● ● ● ● ● ● ● ● ● ● ● ● ●

The Most Unusual Surnames

Strange but true – every one of these surnames was given to at least one person in the past!

Acid	Banana	Bloomers	Broomhead
Agony	Barmy	Blotto	Brownhat
Allchin	Basin	Bogie	Budgie
Ant	Bathbun	Bomb	Buffoon
Anthill	Bed	Boobs	Bug
Argument	Bendova	Bottoms	Bulldog
Aspirin	Bigfoot	Botty	Bum
Attack	Bingo	Bouncy	Bunnyface
Average	Biscuit	Bowtie	Bursting
Awkward	Bisto	Bra	Butterfly
Baboon	Blackeye	Brasskettle	Buttocks
Baguette	Blazer	Brasso	Bythesea
Balamb	Blob	Breakfast	Cake
Bald	Blog	Broadband	Chav

Chicken	Dribble	Gumboil	Macaroni
Chips	Drip	Hatful	Mad
Clot	Drivel	Headache	Madman
Coffee	Drybread	Headroom	Manhole
Coffin	Dull	Hedgehog	Mash
Conqueror	Dump	Highbottom	Measles
Crack	Dust	Hitler	Mental
Crackers	Elephant	Hobbit	Minute
Crap	Fab	Honeybum	Moan
Crapper	Fart	Horrible	Mole
Creep	Farty	Idiot	Monkey
Cucumber	Fat	Itchy	Moped
Daft	Fatty	Jam	Moron
Damp	Ferret	Kitten	Mud
Deadbody	Fieldmouse	Lard	Muggle
Deadly	Fool	Lav	Muppet
Deadman	Fortunate	Leak	Murder
Death	Frankenstein	Liar	Nappy
Decay	Freak	Library	Nerd
Demon	Freaky	Lobster	Newt
Dinner	Frothingham	Longbottom	Nice
Dirty	Geek	Loo	Nit
Dodo	Getsick	Loony	Nobody
Domesday	Glue	Loopy	Nogood
Donkey	God	Loser	Pooer
Dragon	Gromit	Lowfat	Porridge

Prawn	Robinhood	Spong	Trousers
Prong	Rosebottom	Spoon	Turnipseed
Pudding	Rottengoose	Spotty	Ugly
Puffparker	Roundabout	Squid	Vest
Python	Rubber	Squirrel	Vile
Quack	Rubbish	Starbuck	Vinegar
Racoon	Sandbag	Sticky	Wack
Rainwater	Sausage	Stinker	Waffle
Nose	Scratchy	Stoat	Washington
Noseworthy	Scum	Strangeman	Wasp
Nude	Shampoo	Stupid	Wham
Nut	Shifty	Sunshine	Whinge
Nutter	Shovebottom	Swine	Whirligig
Nylon	Shufflebottom	Tank	Whiskers
Onions	Sidebottom	Terrible	Wig
Orange	Skunk	Thickbroom	Willibother
Pancake	Slippery	Thing	Windbottom
Pants	Slob	Tights	Windup
Pee	Sneezy	Tintin	Womble
Pelican	Snogglegrass	Toaster	Woof
Phone	Snot	Toffee	Worm
Piano	Socks	Toothache	Yuck
Picnic	Soup	Tortoise	Zebra
Pong	Speedo	Tortoiseshell	Zillion
Poodle	Spider	Trampleasure	
Rhino	Spinach	Trifle	

Top Surnames in Great Britain

1. Smith	11. Johnson
2. Jones	12. Lewis
3. Taylor	13. Walker
4. Williams	14. Robinson
5. Brown	15. Wood
6. Davies	16. Thompson
7. Evans	17. White
8. Wilson	18. Watson
9. Thomas	19. Jackson
10. Roberts	20. Wright

Top Surnames in England

1. Smith
2. Jones
3. Taylor
4. Brown
5. Williams

Top Surnames in Wales

1. Jones
2. Williams
3. Davies
4. Evans
5. Thomas

Top Surnames in Scotland

1. Smith
2. Brown
3. Wilson
4. Robertson
5. Thomson

Top Surnames in Northern Ireland

1. Wilson
2. Campbell
3. Kelly
4. Johnston
5. Moore

The Most Common Surnames for Each Letter of the Alphabet in the UK

A: Adams
B: Brown
C: Cooper
D: Davies

E: Evans
F: Fox
G: Green
H: Harris
I: Ireland
J: Jones
K: King
L: Lewis
M: Martin
N: Nicholson
O: Owen
P: Phillips
Q: Quinn
R: Roberts
S: Smith
T: Taylor
U: Upton
V: Vincent
W: Williams
Y: Young
Z: Zaoui

Surnames from Around the World

Conventions on surnames vary around the world. In Western countries surnames usually come after the first names, but in many East Asian countries they are given first.

USA

1. Smith
2. Johnson
3. Williams
4. Brown
5. Jones
6. Miller
7. Davis
8. García
9. Rodríguez
10. Wilson

Hispanic People in the USA

1. García
2. Rodríguez
3. Martínez
4. Hernández
5. López
6. González

7. Pérez
8. Sánchez
9. Ramírez
10. Torres

Australia

1. Smith
2. Jones
3. Williams
4. Brown
5. Wilson
6. Taylor
7. Johnson
8. White
9. Martin
10. Anderson

Austria

1. Gruber
2. Huber
3. Bauer
4. Wagner
5. Müller
6. Pichler

7. Steiner
8. Moser
9. Mayer
10. Hofer

Belgium

1. Peeters
2. Janssens
3. Maes
4. Jacobs
5. Mertens
6. Willems
7. Claes
8. Goossens
9. Wouters
10. De Smet

Chile

1. González
2. Muñoz
3. Rojas
4. Díaz
5. Pérez
6. Soto

7. Contreras
8. Silva
9. Martínez
10. Sepúlveda

China

A 2006 survey of 296 million Chinese people in 1,110 counties and cities revealed that although more than 4,000 different surnames were recorded, 85 per cent of all Chinese people share just 100 surnames. That means there are 93 million Wángs, 92 million L's and 88 million Zhāngs.

1. Wáng 王
2. Lǐ 李
3. Zhāng 張
4. Liú 劉
5. Chén 陳
6. Yáng 楊
7. Huán 黃
8. Zhào 趙
9. Wú 吳
10. Zhōu 周

Denmark

1. Jensen
2. Nielsen
3. Hansen
4. Pedersen
5. Andersen
6. Christensen
7. Larsen
8. Sørensen
9. Rasmussen
10. Jørgensen

France

1. Martin
2. Bernard
3. Dubois
4. Thomas
5. Robert
6. Richard
7. Petit
8. Durand
9. Leroy
10. Moreau

Germany

1. Müller (Mueller, Möller)
2. Schmidt (Schmitz, Schmitt, Schmid)
3. Schneider
4. Fischer
5. Meyer (Meier, Maier, Mayer)
6. Weber
7. Schulz (Schulze, Scholz)
8. Wagner
9. Becker
10. Hoffmann (Hofmann)

Hungary

1. Nagy
2. Kovács
3. Tóth
4. Szabó
5. Horváth
6. Varga
7. Kiss
8. Molnár
9. Németh
10. Farkas

Ireland

1. Murphy
2. Kelly
3. O'Sullivan
4. Walsh
5. Smith
6. O'Brien
7. Byrne
8. Ryan
9. Fitzgerald
10. O'Connor

Israel

1. Cohen
2. Levi
3. Mizrachi
4. Peretz
5. Biton
6. Dahan
7. Abraham
8. Friedman
9. Azulai
10. Malcah

Italy

1. Rossi
2. Russo
3. Ferrari
4. Esposito
5. Bianchi
6. Romano
7. Colombo
8. Ricci
9. Marino
10. Greco

Japan

1. Satō 佐藤
2. Suzuki 鈴木
3. Takahashi 高橋
4. Tanaka 田中
5. Watanabe 渡辺 (渡邉)
6. Itō 伊藤
7. Yamamoto 山本
8. Nakamura 中村
9. Kobayashi 小林
10. Saitō 斎藤 (斉藤)

Norway, 2009

1. Hansen
2. Johansen
3. Olsen
4. Larsen
5. Andersen
6. Pedersen
7. Nilsen
8. Kristiansen
9. Jensen
10. Karlsen

Poland

1. Nowak
2. Kowalski
3. Wisniewski
4. Wójcik
5. Kowalczyk
6. Kaminski
7. Lewandowski
8. Zielinski
9. Szymanski
10. Wozniak

Russia

1. **Smirnov** – Смирнов
2. **Ivanov** – Иванов
3. **Kuznetsov** – Кузнецов
4. **Popov** – Попов
5. **Sokolov** – Соколов
6. **Lebedev** – Лебедев
7. **Kozlov** – Козлов
8. **Novikov** – Новиков
9. **Morozov** – Морозов
10. **Petrov** – Петров

Singapore

1. **Tan** 陈 (陳)
2. **Lim** 林
3. **Lee** 李
4. **Ng** 黄
5. **Ong** 王
6. **Wong** 黃
7. **Goh** 吳
8. **Chua** 蔡
9. **Chan** 陈 (陳)
10. **Koh** 许 (許)

Spain

1. García
2. Fernández
3. González
4. Rodríguez
5. López
6. Martínez
7. Sánchez
8. Pérez
9. Martín
10. Gómez

Sweden

1. Johansson
2. Andersson
3. Karlsson
4. Nilsson
5. Eriksson
6. Larsson
7. Olsson
8. Persson
9. Svensson
10. Gustafsson

Say (and Spell) It Correctly!

Some surnames are not pronounced as you might think – there are some variations, but these are the usual ways:

Althorpe *al-thrup*
Ayscough *askew*
Bagehot *baggot*
Balfour *bal-fer*
Beauchamp *beech-um*
Buccleuch *buck-loo*
Cholmondeley *chumly*
Colquhoun *ca-hoon*
Copland *copeland*
Cowper *coop-er*
Dalziel *deal* or *dee-ell*
Death *deeth*
Donne *dunn*
Ehle *ee-lee*
Featherstonehaugh *fanshaw*
Fiennes *fines*
Geoghegan *gaygan*
Grosvenor *grove-ner*
Harewood *harwood*
Home *hume*

Jacques *jakes*
Keynes *kaynz*
Lauren *lorr-en*
Leicester *lester*
Looney *low-nee*
Mainwaring *mannering*
Marjoribanks *marchbanks*
Maugham *mawm*
Maurice *morris*
Menzies *ming-iss*
Pepys *peeps*
St Clair *sink-lur*
St John *sin-jun*
Strachan *strawn*
Tatham *tate-um*
Urquhart *ur-cut*
Worcester *wooster*
Wriothesley *roxly*
Yeats *yates*

3. FULL NAMES

· · · · · · · · · · · · · ·

The Most Common Full names in England & Wales

Men

1. David Jones
2. David Smith
3. John Smith
4. David Williams
5. Michael Smith
6. John Jones
7. John Williams
8.= Paul Smith 8.= Peter Smith
10. David Evans
11. Robert Smith
12. Andrew Smith
13. James Smith
14. Robert Jones
15. John Taylor
16. John Davies
17. David Brown
18. David Thomas

19. Michael Jones
20. David Davies

Women

1. Margaret Smith
2. Margaret Jones
3. Susan Smith
4. Susan Jones
5. Mary Smith
6. Patricia Smith
7. Margaret Williams
8. Elizabeth Jones
9. Mary Jones
10. Sarah Jones
11. Elizabeth Smith
12. Sarah Smith
13. Jean Smith
14. Margaret Davies
15. Christine Smith
16. Joan Smith
17. Susan Williams
18. Patricia Jones
19. Margaret Taylor
20. Margaret Brown

Unusual couples!

Sometimes when two people get married, they will join their surnames together rather than picking one or the other – occasionally with amusing results!

Bacon–Roll

Annie Bacon married Oliver Roll, Wandsworth, London, June 2003

Beach–Ball

John Beach married Jane Ball, St Pancras, London, 16 August 1825

Beard–Shaver
Harriet Beard married Madison Shaver, Rowan, North Carolina, USA, 25 December 1865

Bird–Brain
George Isaac Bird married Alice Brain, Bristol, Gloucestershire, 25 December 1890

Brain–Box
Jemima Brain married William Box, Shipston-on-Stour, Warwickshire, 1912

Cannon–Ball
Ann Cannon married John Ball, St Saviour's, Southwark, London, 1830

Carr–Driver
Tommie Levada Carr married Jemmy Ray Driver,
Putnam, Tennessee, USA, 23 December 1967

Carr–Park
David H. Carr married Ethel F. Park,
Barrow-in-Furness, Cumbria, 1913

Cat–Dog
John Cat married Bessie Dog, Bennett,
South Dakota, USA, 29 May 1921

Cock–Roach
Hannah Cock married Thomas Roach,
Burnley, Lancashire, 1912

Day–Light
Elizabeth M. Day married Albert F. Light,
Edmonton, Middlesex, 1919

Fish–Pye
Elizabeth Fish married Charles Pye, Bolton, Lancashire, 1927

Flower–Power
Carl E. V. Flower married Rebecca B. J. Power,
Dudley, West Midlands, 1996

Good–Bye
Robert Good married Elizabeth Bye,
Haywood, Tennessee, USA, 8 July 1963

Goody–Goody
Jill E. Goody married David D. Goody, Halifax, Yorkshire, 1986

Hammer–Nail

Mary Hammer married Andrew Jackson Nail,
Shelby, Texas, USA, 1839

Hand–Baggs

William G. Hand married Mildred Baggs,
Wimborne, Dorset, 1925

James–Bond

John James married Margaret Bond,
Chesterfield, Derbyshire, 1913

King–Kong

Jeremy B. King married Rosalyn L. Kong,
Sodbury, Gloucestershire, 1989

Large–Butt

Lottie L. Large married Francis H. Butt,
Cirencester, Gloucestershire, 1913

Little–Large

Kathleen Little married George Large,
Bristol, Gloucestershire, 1921

Lock–Key

Hannah Lock married Richard Key,
Covent Garden, London, 31 May 1800

Long–Short

William A. Long married Nancy Gentry
Short, Vernon, Missouri, USA, 22 August 1877

McDonald–Burger

Frederick McDonald married Elizabeth Burger,
New York, USA, 1793

Money–Penny

Ernest J. Money married Annie S. Penny,
Chorlton, Lancashire, 1922

Night–Day

George Night married Susan Day, Whitley,
Kentucky, USA, 4 June 1820

Quack–Quack

Margaret E. Quack married Harold H. K. Quack,
Liverpool, Lancashire, 1913

Rich–Poor

Henry Rich married Elizabeth Poor,
Boston, Massachusetts, America, 1 October 1705

Rude–Bottom

Andrew O. Rude married Jean E. Bottom,
Riverside, California, USA, 7 June 1969

Sargeant–Major

Edwin Sargeant married Catherine R. Major,
Brentford, Middlesex, 1912

Seymour–Bottom

William Seymour married Jane Bottom,
Wandsworth, London, 1912

Sherlock–Holmes
John Sherlock married Florence Holmes,
Wolstanton, Staffordshire, 1921

Short–Tall
Jane Short married John Tall, Winchester,
Hampshire, 21 January 1832

Snow–Mann

Florence M. Snow married Conrad A. Mann,
Tendring, Essex, 1919

Sun–Tan

Jian H. Sun married Koi E. Tan, Lewes, East Sussex, 2003

Wise–Guy

George Wise married Daisy Guy, Fulham, London, 1915

Whyte–Pants

Joyce Whyte married Rogar [sic] Pants,
Allhallows London Wall, 7 October 1652

Wright–Wong

Billy D. Wright married Vanessa J. Wong,
Tunbridge Wells, Kent, 1988

Strange-sounding Names

Barb Dwyer
Pearl Button
Hazel Nutt
Ray Gunn
Helen Back
Stan Still
Jo King
Lee King
Terry Bull
Mary Christmas
Max Power

Page Turner
Sunny Day
Tim Burr
Teresa Green
Will Power
Anna Sasin
Chris Cross
Doug Hole

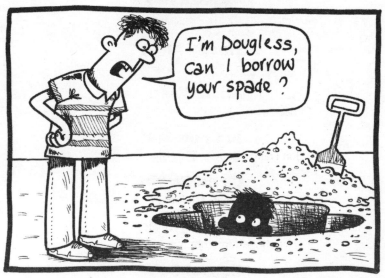

Justin Case
Barry Cade
Sue Mee

AKA – Also Known As . . .

The Real Names of Famous People

Many writers, actors, singers and others in the public eye change their names for a variety of reasons – for example, to make them more memorable, easier to say, or to avoid sounding too similar to another person's name. These are just a few of thousands of names of famous people that are not the ones with which they were born:

Muhammad Ali
Cassius Marcellus Clay (1942–), boxer

Woody Allen
Allen Stewart Konigsberg (1935–), film actor/director

Cilla Black
Priscilla White (1943–), singer/TV presenter

Jon Bon Jovi
Jon Francis Bongiovi, Jr. (1962–), rock star

David Bowie
David Robert Hayward-Jones (1947–), singer

Nicolas Cage
Nicholas Kim Coppola (1964–), actor

Michael Caine
Maurice Micklewhite (1933–), actor

Lewis Carroll
Charles Lutwidge Dodgson (1832–98),
Alice in Wonderland author

Agatha Christie

Mary Westmacott (1890–1976), author of
Poirot and *Miss Marple* mysteries

Tom Cruise

Thomas Cruise Mapother IV (1962–), actor

Miley Cyrus

Destiny Hope Cyrus (1992–), singer/actress

Vin Diesel

Mark Vincent (1967–), actor

Snoop Dogg

Calvin Broadus, Jr. (1971–), rapper/actor/producer

Dr Dre

Andre Young (1965–), rap artist

Bob Dylan

Robert Allen Zimmerman (1941–), folk singer

Ms Dynamite

Niomi McLean-Daley (1981–), singer

Missy Elliott

Melissa Arnette Elliott (1971–), singer

50 Cent

Curtis Jackson (1975–), rap artist

Whoopi Goldberg

Caryn Johnson (1955–), comedian/actress

Cary Grant
Archibald Leach (1904–86), actor

Macy Gray
Natalie McIntyre (1967–), singer

Sir Elton John
Reginald Kenneth Dwight (1947–), singer

Alicia Keys
Alicia Augello Cook (1981–), singer

Ashton Kutcher
Christopher Kutcher (1978–), actor

Queen Latifah
Dana Elaine Owens (1970–), singer/actress

Ralph Lauren
Ralph Lipschitz (1939–), fashion designer

Jude Law
David Jude Heyworth Law (1972–), actor

Elle Macpherson
Eleanor Gow (1963–), model/actress

Marilyn Manson
Brian Warner (1969–), rock musician

Freddie Mercury
Farouk Bulsara (1946–91), rock singer

Marilyn Monroe
Norma Jean Baker (1926–62), actress

Demi Moore
Demetria Guynes (1962–), actress

Billie Piper
Lianne Paul Piper (1982–), singer/actress

Iggy Pop
James Newell Osterberg Jr (1947–), punk singer

Busta Rhymes
Trevor Tahiem Smith, Jr. (1972–), rap artist

Cliff Richard
Harold Rodger Webb (1940–), singer/actor

Meg Ryan
Margaret Hyra (1961–), actress

Dr Seuss
Theodore Seuss Geisel (1904–91), author of *The Cat in the Hat* and *How the Grinch Stole Christmas*

Frank Skinner
Chris Collins (1957–), comedian

Lemony Snicket
Daniel Handler (1970–), author of *A Series of Unfortunate Events*

Ringo Starr
Richard Starkey (1940–), drummer with The Beatles

David Tennant
David McDonald (1971–), *Doctor Who* actor

Mark Twain
Samuel Langhorne Clemens (1835–1910),
author of *Tom Sawyer* and *Huckleberry Finn*

Sid Vicious
John Simon Ritchie (1957–79), punk musician

John Wayne
Marion Morrison (1907–79), actor

Stevie Wonder
Stevland Hardaway Morris/Judkins (1950–), singer

Tiger Woods
Eldrick Woods (1975–), golf champion

● ● ● ● ● ● ● ● ● ● ● ● ● ● ●

Initial Impressions

Some people prefer to go by their initials
instead of their full names.

W. H. (Wystan Hugh) Auden
Poet

Rev. W. (Wilbert) Awdry
Author of the *Thomas the Tank Engine* stories

J. M. (James Matthew) Barrie
Author of *Peter Pan*

L. (Lyman) Frank Baum
Author of *The Wonderful Wizard of Oz*

W. E. B. (Wilian Edward Burghardt) Du Bois
Academic and civil rights activist

T. S. (Thomas Stearns) Eliot
Poet who wrote the book on which the musical *Cats* was based

P. J. (Polly Jean) Harvey
Musician

K. D. (Kathryn Dawn) Lang
Singer

D. H. (David Herbert) Lawrence
Author

T. E. (Thomas Edward) Lawrence
Soldier/writer, 'Lawrence of Arabia'

C. S. (Clive Staples) Lewis
Author of *The Chronicles of Narnia*

A. A. (Alan Alexander) Milne
Author of the *Winnie-the-Pooh* stories

E. (Edith) Nesbit
Author of *Five Children and It* and *The Railway Children*

J. K. (Joanne Kathleen) Rowling
Author of the *Harry Potter* series

W. H. (William Henry) Smith
English businessman and founder of a
chain of newsagents and bookshops

R. L. (Robert Lawrence) Stine
Goosebumps author

J. R. R. (John Ronald Reuel) Tolkien
Author of *The Hobbit* and *The Lord of the Rings*

J. M. W. (Joseph Mallord William) Turner
Landscape painter

H. G. (Herbert George) Wells
Science-fiction author of *The War of the Worlds*
and *The Time Machine*

E. B. (Elwyn Brooks) White
Charlotte's Web and *Stuart Little* author

• • • • • • • • • • • • • • •

Palindromic Names

Palindromes – sentences, words or, in this case, names
spelled the same backwards as forwards. For example, in
early 19th-century America, Harrah Reynolds married
Hannah Wells – both had palindromic first names, and
they had 12 children to whom they also gave palindromic
names: Hannah, Asa, Emme, Iri, Anna, Aziza, Zerez,
Axa, Atta, Alila, Numun and Harrah

Some other examples:

Anna Danna
(1921–2008, Louisiana, USA)

Opal M. Lapo
(Born Michigan, USA, c. 1906)

Otto Rentner
(1902–72, California, USA)

Revilo Oliver
(1908–94, Illinois, USA)

Tom Mot
(1906–90, Colchester, Essex)

Nebelow Woleben
(19th-century Illinois, USA)

Ronnoc Connor
(1903–72, Illinois, USA)

Lon Nol
Prime minister of Cambodia (1913–85)

Norabel LeBaron
(1907–10, Michigan, USA)

Mike Kim
(1976–), Korean author

Robert Trebor
(1953–) American actor (who made his name a
palindrome when picking his stage name!)

Yendis Sidney
(Born West Ham, Essex, 1990)

Neil Lien
(1883–1964, Wisconsin, USA)

● ● ● ● ● ● ● ● ● ● ● ● ● ● ●

Puritan Names

The Puritans of the late 16th and early 17th centuries
were extreme Protestants who often chose names
that expressed some virtue or religious slogan.
Here are a few of the more unusual ones . . .

Nicholas If-Jesus-Christ-Had-Not-Died-For-Thee-Thou-Hadst-Been-Damned Barebon
Born London c.1640; died Osterley, Middlesex, 1698

Magnify Beard
Baptized Warbleton, Sussex, 17 September 1587

Lament Bible
Married Nicholas Hussher, Ticehurst,
Sussex, 9 September 1640

Be-Courteous Cole
Born Pevensey, Sussex, 1570

Diligence Constant
Buried St Peter upon Cornhill, London, 1 November 1724

God-Help Cooper
Baptized Weybridge, Surrey, 12 June 1628

Sorry-for-Sin Coupard
Baptized Warbleton, Sussex, 25 January 1589

Abuse-Not Ellis
Baptized Warbleton, Sussex, 17 September 1592

Joy-in-Sorrow Godman
Married Joseph Baysie, All Saints',
Lewes, Sussex, 20 May 1614

Hate-Evil Greenhill
Baptized Banbury, Oxfordshire, 15 April 1660

Sin-Deny Hely
(Female) Married William Swane,
Burwash, Sussex, 4 September 1621

Safe-on-High Hopkinson
Baptized Salehurst, Sussex, 28 February 1591

First-Borne and Sadness Luffe
(Female twins) Baptized Aylesbury,
Buckinghamshire, 2 September 1656

Free-Gift and Fear-Not Lulham
(Male twins) Baptized Warbleton, Sussex, 12 October 1589

Hate Evil Nutter
Born England 1603; died Dover,
New Hampshire, America, 28 June 1675

Abstinence Pougher
(Male) Baptized St Nicholas', Leicester, 30 June 1672

More-Fruit Stone
(Male) Baptized Alfriston, Sussex, 6 June 1587

No-Merit Vynall
(Female) Baptized Warbleton, Sussex, 28 September 1589

Continent Walker
(Female) Baptized Alfriston, Sussex, 22 December 1594

Restored Weekes
Married Constant Sumar, Chiddingly, Sussex, 27 August 1618

Faint-Not Wood
Married William Clarke, Laughton, Sussex, 24 December 1618

Repentance Wrath
(Male) Baptized Elham, Kent, 26 March 1612

What the Dickens?
Charles Dickens's Strangest Character Names

The great British writer Charles Dickens (1812–70) created and named almost 1,000 characters in his books and stories. Some of them were based on real people with the same or similar names; others might have been people whose names he had seen in newspapers, but many were invented.

Some of these have entered the English language – 'Scrooge' from Ebenezer Scrooge, the miser in *A Christmas Carol*, is the name often given to other mean people; Fagin, the villain in *Oliver Twist*, is used to describe the leader of a criminal gang; and Dolly Varden from *Barnaby Rudge* gave her name to a style of dress and hat.

Quebec Bagnet *(Bleak House)*
Lord Decimus Tite Barnacle
(Little Dorrit)
Henrietta Boffin *(Our Mutual Friend)*
Conkey Chickweed *(Oliver Twist)*
Major Hannibal Chollop
(Martin Chuzzlewit)
Diggory Chuzzlewit
(Martin Chuzzlewit)
Canon Septimus Crisparkle
(The Mystery of Edwin Drood)
Alderman Cute
(Christmas Books, 'The Chimes')

Volumnia Dedlock *(Bleak House)*
Nicodemus Dumps *(Sketches by Boz,*
'The Bloomsbury Christening')
Affery Flintwich *(Little Dorrit)*
Hiram Grewgious
(The Mystery of Edwin Drood)
Luke Honeythunder
(The Mystery of Edwin Drood)
Caddy Jellyby *(Bleak House)*
Augustus Moddle *(Martin Chuzzlewit)*
Newman Noggs *(Nicholas Nickleby)*
Mercy Pecksniff *(Martin Chuzzlewit)*
Dot Peerybingle *(Christmas Books, 'The*
Cricket on the Hearth')
John Podsnap *(Our Mutual Friend)*
Uncle Pumblechook
(Great Expectations)
Professor Pumpkinskull
(The Mudfog and Other Sketches)
Pleasant Riderhood
(Our Mutual Friend)
Zephania Scadder *(Martin Chuzzlewit)*
Sloppy *(Our Mutual Friend)*
Chevy Slyme *(Martin Chuzzlewit)*
Wackford Squeers *(Nicholas Nickleby)*
Phil Squod *(Bleak House)*

Paul Sweedlepipe *(Martin Chuzzlewit)*
Dick Swiveller *(The Old Curiosity Shop)*
Polly Toodle *(Dombey and Son)*
Lucretia Tox *(Dombey and Son)*
Prince Turveydrop *(Bleak House)*
Anastasia Veneering *(Our Mutual Friend)*
Silas Wegg *(Our Mutual Friend)*
Wopsle *(Great Expectations)*

• • • • • • • • • • • • • •

Randomized List of Strange First Names and Surnames

I shuffled my list of strange first names with my list of surnames and paired them up – why not see what unusual combinations you can come up with?

First name	Surname
Emperor	Geek
Tesco	Mash
Three	Spong
Muppet	Fortunate
Oxygen	Tintin
Lasagna	Gromit
President	Windup
Absolutely	Bra
Frightful	Elephant

Lollipop	Puffparker
Tornado	Banana
Goblin	Fool
Halloween	Bum
Mole	Rosebottom
Dumbo	Breakfast
Pudding	Bug
Marmalade	Whiskers
Dynamite	Headache

Tomato	Noseworthy
Cheese	Wack
Peculiar	Muppet
Pickles	Nice
Fridge	Dump
Landrover	Broomhead
Custard	Fatty
Atomic	Murder
Honk	Mental
Arsenal	Slob
Preserved	Nut
Bad	Brownhat
Absurd	Tights
Spider	Thing
Gaga	Loony
Sardine	Hatful
Giraffe	Mad
Telegraph	Argument
Rhubarb	Rainwater
Fatty	Dinner
Gravy	Biscuit
Christmas	Fieldmouse
Mad	Swine
Floppy	Macaroni
Elastic	Moped
Argos	Bouncy

Avatar	Crap
Fairy	Skunk
Eggy	Trousers
Ostrich	Conqueror
Excellent	Pancake
Badger	Scratchy
Crash	Quack
Kangaroo	Bogie
Geek	Hedgehog
Thousand	Blazer
Bash	Headroom
Million	Deadman
Sloth	Womble
Snowman	Rhino
Zebra	Nobody
Armadillo	Idiot
Burp	Toaster
Submarine	Domesday
Banana	Acid
Lemonade	Brasskettle
Dangerous	Cake
Uranus	Bloomers
Electric	Ugly
Fish	Agony
Trainers	Sunshine
Famous	Tortoise

Blog	Chimp
Death	Walnut
Strangeman	Fat
Attack	Poo
Orange	Handy
Bomb	Creature
Terrible	Botty
Dust	Agony
Stinker	Chicken
Liar	Nutella
Baboon	Nasty
Blotto	Bomb
Dirty	Elephant
Windbottom	Pants
Bathbun	Duvet
Blob	Quack
Damp	Aspirin
Average	Toilet
Nogood	Farty
Loopy	Emu
Drip	Sandwich
Blackeye	Thirteen
Snot	Dirty
Horrible	Pig
Buffoon	Wardrobe
Fart	Ipad

Odd	Dodo
Angry	Bald
Thick	Bythesea
Hamster	Bingo
Belch	Boobs
Bat	Racoon
Chutney	Robinhood
Volcano	Ant
Hobbit	Awkward
Jelly	Hitler
Cupboard	Crapper
Fang	Coffee
Adder	Fat
Cod	Deadbody
Eel	Chips
Hippo	Wig
Audi	Freaky
Blender	Spotty
Daft	Wham
Teapot	Longbottom
Toffee	Itchy
Toast	Allchin
Bogey	Frankenstein
Muffin	Whinge
Horrible	Kitten
Ginger	Jam

Abba	Leak
Salami	God
Banger	Baguette
Monster	Pooer
Birdseye	Drivel
Cuckoo	Cucumber
Idiot	Woof
Blackberry	Monkey
Otter	Stupid
Choochoo	Pee
Ah	Butterfly
Albatross	Creep
Quasimodo	Washington
Dim	Spider
Encyclopedia Britannica	Muggle
Camel	Trampleasure
Treacle	Crack
Murder	Nappy
Bovril	Scum
Birmingham	Mole
Baboon	Nerd
Dolphin	Lav
Biscuit	Toothache
Cool	Gumboil
Muck	Broadband
Evil	Manhole

Auk	Sandbag
Oyster	Frothingham
Awful	Newt
Cement	Prong
Jedward	Bunnyface
Pringles	Crackers
Marmite	Wasp
Watercress	Python
Carpet	Soup
Limousine	Pants

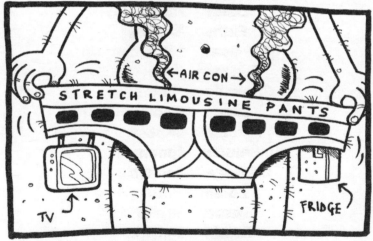

Zonk	Waffle
Gnome	Pudding
Professor	Stoat
Whalebelly	Vile

Blood	Hobbit
Bounce	Socks
Pirate	Zebra
Bacardi	Moan
Hairy	Freak
Thirty	Slippery
Chocolate	Nutter
Hopeless	Piano
Jam	Mud
Doctor	Loo
Baldy	Farty
Filthy	Rubbish
Goat	Nit
Earless	Yuck
Skeleton	Phone
Bendy	Nylon
Zip	Dribble
University	Spoon
Cabbage	Honeybum
Zoom	Highbottom
Lizard	Drybread
Vermin	Shovebottom
Bubble	Dragon
Crazy	Barmy
Ugly	Balamb
Scary	Bursting

Gorilla	Sneezy
Cricket	Donkey
Swine	Lard
Cash	Daft
Turkey	Shampoo
Billion	Tank
Mustard	Trifle
Grasshopper	Glue
Hitler	Budgie
Freak	Buttocks
Enormous	Bed
Sick	Demon
Trouser	Toffee
Bottle	Bowtie
Alien	Spinach

4. NICKNAMES

• • • • • • • • • • • • •

People Best Known by Their Nicknames

The Big Bopper

US singer Jiles Perry Richardson Jr (1930–59)

Billy the Kid

US outlaw William H. Bonney/McCarty (1859–81)

Braveheart

Scottish leader Sir William Wallace (c.1274–1305)

Butch Cassidy

US outlaw Robert LeRoy Parker (1866–1908),
partner-in-crime of the Sundance Kid

El Cid

Spanish hero Rodrigo Díaz de Vivar (c.1043–99);
his nickname means 'The Lord'

El Greco

Greek painter Domenico Theotocopuli (1541–1614);
his nickname, which means 'The Greek', was used
because his real name was difficult to pronounce

The Rock

US wrestler/actor Dwayne Douglas Johnson (born 1972)

The Sundance Kid

US outlaw Harry Longabaugh (1860–1909),
partner-in-crime of Butch Cassidy

Unfortunate Royal Nicknames

Monarchs are not always popular figures, as one can imagine
from some of the nicknames they seem to attract!

Alfonso the Fat

Alfonso II, king of Portugal (reigned 1212–23)

Charles the Bad

Charles II, king of Navarre (reigned 1349–87)

Charles the Bald

Charles I, king of France (reigned 840–77)

Charles the Mad

Charles VI, king of France (reigned 1380–1422)

Charles the Simple

Charles III, king of France (reigned 893–929)

Christian the Cruel

Christian II of Denmark and Norway (reigned 1513–23)
*He cruelly massacred people in Sweden, which
he also ruled after 1520, but died in jail.*

Constantine the Copronymus

Constantine V, Byzantine emperor (reigned 741–75)
*When he was christened in 718, he pooed into the font
(copronymus means 'one who poos'!).*

Fulk the Surly

Fulk IV, count of Anjou (reigned 1068–1109)

Ivan the Terrible

Ivan IV, tsar of Russia (reigned 1533–84)
*Got his nickname for his habit of torturing animals.
He later massacred many people, and even killed
his own son in a rage.*

Louis the Cruel
Louis XI of France (reigned 1461–83)
*Also known as the Universal Spider, he was
involved in many plots and murders.*

Louis the Fat
Louis VI, king of France (reigned 1108–37)

Louis the Sluggard
Louis V, king of France (reigned 986–7)

Pedro the Cruel
King of Castile (reigned 1350–69)
He assassinated many of his opponents.

Sancho the Fat
Sancho I of León (reigned 956–65)
*They didn't call him fat for nothing – apparently he was so fat,
he could not walk without being supported!*

Sebastian the Madman
Sebastian of Portugal (reigned 1557–78)
A boy-king who led his country into disastrous battles.

Selim the Grim
Selim I, Turkish sultan (reigned 1512–20)
*This sultan murdered 40,000 religious opponents (so you
might wonder if 'grim' is quite strong enough a word).*

William the Bad
William I of Sicily (reigned 1154–66)
*His reign was marked by disasters – but he
was succeeded by William the Good!*

Criminal Nicknames

Al Capone, a notorious gangster who operated mainly in Chicago during the 1920s, was given the nickname 'Scarface' after a fight outside a nightclub left him with visible scars. FBI records show that many other criminals chose to go by nicknames, and all of these names belonged to real American criminals during the early part of the 20th century – although we can only guess at how some of these names were earned.

Men

Airbrake Smith
Am I Blue
Ammunition Shorty
Ant Eater
Bad Eggs
Banjo Eyes
Big Lip Louie
Box Car Casey
Brief Case Kid
Bughouse Bill
Cake Eater
Carbolic Kid
Charley Low Down
Charlie Kick-the-Door-In
Clothes Line Slim
Cream Puffs

Crying Shame
Dill Pickle
Diphtheria Jack
Ex Ray Kid
Fog Horn Kelly
Gold Tooth Frenchy
Izzy the Eel
Piccolo Pete
Rooster face

Schuffle Dirty
Silk Hat Harry
Slow But Sure
Soup House Pete

Stick in the Mud
The Fighting Butcher
Tomato Slim

Women

Babbling Bess
Belching Blanche
Bowlegged Bessie
Cigar Kate
Dare-Devil Billie
Fanny the Hop
Iron Foot Florence
National Park Mary
Shoe String Mary
Three Finger Liz
Wild Cat Alma

Sporting Nicknames

Boxers

The Beast from the East
Nikolay Valuev

Clones Cyclone
Barry McGuigan

The Executioner
Bernard Hopkins

The Haymaker
David Haye

The Hitman
Ricky Hatton

Iron Mike
Mike Tyson

Louisville Lip
Muhammad Ali

Pac-Man
Manny Pacquaio

The Pride of Wales
Joe Calzaghe

Prince
Naseem Hamed

Real Deal
Evander Holyfield

Smokin' Joe
Joe Frazier

Cricketers

Banger
Marcus Trescothick

Beefy
Sir Ian Botham

Bloodaxe
Mark Ramprakash

Bunions
Graham Onions

The Cat
Phil Tufnell

The Don
Don Bradman

The Haryana Hurricane
Kapil Dev

The King of Spin
Shane Warne

Punter
Ricky Ponting

The Sikh of Tweak
Monty Panesar

Westlife
Stuart Broad

Whispering Death
Michael Holding

Darts Players

The Artist
Kevin Painter

Bravedart
Jamie Harvey

The Crafty Cockney
Eric Bristow

Darth Maple
John Part

The Hammer
Andy Hamilton

The Heat
Denis Ovens

The Iceman
Alan Warriner-Little

Jackpot
Adrian Lewis

The King; Merve the Swerve
Mervyn King

The Menace
Dennis Priestley

Old Stoneface
John Lowe

The Power
Phil Taylor

The Prince of Style
Rod Harrington

The Rocket
Ronnie Baxter

The Viking
Andy Fordham

The Wizard
Colin Osborne

Football Players

Baby-faced Assassin
Ole Gunner Solskjær

The Bison
Michael Essien

Boa Constrictor
Luís Boa Morte

Crazy Horse
Emlyn Hughes

Danger Defoe
Jermaine Defoe

Der Kaiser
Franz Beckenbauer

Gazza
Paul Gascoigne

The Giraffe or Bean Pole
Peter Crouch

Goldenballs
David Beckham

The Golden Bomber
Jürgen Klinsmann

The Golden Boy
Kaká

The Non-flying Dutchman
Dennis Bergkamp

Psycho
Stuart Pearce

Roadrunner
Aaron Lennon

Sparky
Mark Hughes

Va Va Voom
Thierry Henry

Snooker Players

The Captain
Ali Carter

Dracula
Ray Reardon

The Fen Potter
Joe Perry

The Golden Boy
Stephen Hendry

The Grinder
Cliff Thorburn

Hong Kong Fu-ey
Marco Fu

The Hurricane
Alex Higgins

The Jester from Leicester
Mark Selby

The Melbourne Machine
Neil Robertson

The Nugget
Steve Davis

The Pocket Dynamo
Graeme Dott

Rocket
Ronnie O'Sullivan

Sheriff of Pottingham
Anthony Hamilton

The Stoke Potter
Dave Harold

The Thai-Phoon
James Wattana

The Welsh Dragon
Matthew Stevens

The Whirlwind
Jimmy White

Wizard of Wishaw
John Higgins

Wrestlers

The Big Show
Paul Wight, Jr

Edge
Adam Joseph Copeland

The Miz
Mike Mizanin

Triple H
Paul Michael Levesque

The Undertaker
Mark William Calaway

Golfers

Big Easy
Ernie Els

Boom Boom
Fred Couples

The Golden Bear
Jack Nicklaus

The Goose
Retief Goosen

The Great White Shark
Greg Norman

Tennis Players

Fed-Ex
Roger Federer

The King of Clay
Rafa Nadal

Pistol Pete
Pete Sampras

Rocket Man
Andy Roddick

Swiss Maid
Martina Hingis

Others

Big Cactus
Shaquille O'Neal (basketball)

Blade Runner
Oscar Pistorius (Paralympic sprinter)

The Boss
Lance Armstrong (cycling)

The Doctor
Valentino Rossi (MotoGP)

The Refrigerator
William Perry (American Football)

Comic Superheroes' Real Names

You can't be a superhero without a cool-sounding alias! Here is a selection some of the most famous comic superheroes along with their real names, and the year they were first created.

Some of these heroes have been recreated with different names over the years (in the Batman comics, the name 'Robin' has now been used by five different people), but these are all the original characters to use the name.

Ant-Man
Dr Henry 'Hank' Pym (1962)

Bananaman
Eric Twinge (1980)

Batgirl/Oracle
Barbara Gordon (1961)

Batman
Bruce Wayne (1939)

Beast
Hank McCoy (1963)

Captain Action
Clive Arno (1968)

Captain America
Steve Rogers (1941)

Captain Marvel
William Joseph 'Billy' Batson (1940)

Colossus
Piotr Rasputin (1975)

The Comet
John Dickering (1940)

Cyclops
Scott Summers (1963)

Daredevil
Matthew Michael 'Matt' Murdock (1964)

Mr Fantastic
Reed Richards (1961)

Firestorm
Ronnie Raymond (1978)

The Flash
Jay Garrick (1940)

Green Arrow
Oliver Jonas 'Ollie' Queen (1941)

The Green Hornet
Britt Reid (1936)

Green Lantern
Alan Scott (1940)

Hawkeye
Clint Barton (1964)

He-Man
Prince Adam of Eternia (1981)

The Hulk
Robert Bruce Banner (1962)

The Human Torch
Johnny Storm (1961)

Iceman
Robert 'Bobby' Louis Drake (1963)

Invisible Girl/Woman
Susan Storm Richards (1961)

Iron Man
Anthony Edward 'Tony' Stark (1963)

Judge Dredd
Joseph Dredd (1977)

Magneto
Max Eisenhardt/Erik Lehnsher (1963)

Marvel Girl
Rachel Anne Summers (1981)

Mary Marvel
Mary Willow Batson (1942)

The Phantom
Kit Walker (1936)

Plasticman
Patrick 'Eel' O'Brian (1941)

Power Girl
Karen Starr (1976)

Professor X
Charles Xavier (1963)

Robin
Dick Grayson (1940)

The Shadow
Lamont Cranston (1930)

Spawn
Albert Francis 'Al' Simmons (1992)

She-Hulk
Jennifer Susan Walters (1980)

Spectre
Jim Corrigan (1940)

Spider-Girl
May Parker (1998)

Spider-Man
Peter Parker (1962)

Storm
Ororo Munroe (1975)

Supergirl
Kara Zor-El/Linda Lee Danvers (1950)

Superman
Kal-El/Clark Kent (1938)

The Thing
Benjamin Jacob Grimm (1961)

Wolverine

James Howlett (1974)

Wonder Woman

Diana Prince (1941)

● ● ● ● ● ● ● ● ● ● ● ● ● ●

One-name People

Here are some well-known people who prefer to
go by just the one name!

Aaliyah

Singer/actress; Aaliyah Haughton (1979–2001)

Banksy

Graffiti artist; true identity unknown)

Barbie

Doll; Barbara Millicent Roberts (1959–)

Beyoncé

Singer; Beyoncé Knowles (1981–)

Björk

Icelandic singer/actress; Björk Guömundsdóttir (1965–)

Bono

Rock band U2 singer; Paul Hewson (1960–)

Canaletto

Italian painter; Giovanni Antonio Canal (1697–1768)

Cher
Singer; Cherilyn Sarkisian (1946–)

Colette
French writer; Sidonie-Gabrielle Colette (1873–1954)

Coolio
Rapper; Artis Leon Ivey, Jr (1963–)

Dido
Singer; Florian Cloud de Bounevialle Armstrong (1971–)

Eminem
Rap singer; Marshall Mathers (1972–)

Enya
Irish singer; Eithne ní Bhraonáin (1961–)

Evita
Argentinean politician; Eva Perón (1919–52)

Flea
Red Hot Chili Peppers bass guitarist;
Michael Peter Balzary (1962–)

Goldie
Musician; Clifford Joseph Price (1965–)

Hergé
Tintin cartoonist; Georges Rémi (1907–83)

Houdini
Magician; Erich Weiss (1874–1926)

Lulu
Singer; Marie McDonald McLaughlin Lawrie (1948–)

Madonna
Singer; Madonna Louise Ciccone (1958–)

Meat Loaf
Singer; Marvin/Michael Lee Aday (1947–)

Michelangelo
Italian painter; Michelangelo Buonarroti (1475–1564)

Moby
Musician; Richard Melville Hall (1965–)

Pelé
Brazilian footballer; Edson Arantes do Nascimento (1940–)

Pink
Singer; Alecia Moore (1979–)

Prince
Musician; Prince Rogers Nelson (1958–)

Ronaldhino
Brazilian footballer; Ronaldo de Assis Moreira (1980–)

Ronaldo
Brazilian footballer; Ronaldo Luís Nazário de Lima (1976–)

Shaggy
Jamaican singer; Orville Richard Burrell (1968–)

Sting
Singer; Gordon Matthew Sumner (1951–)

Tintoretto
Italian painter; Jacopo Comin (1518–94)

Twiggy
Model; Lesley Hornby (1949–)

Voltaire
French writer; François-Marie Arouet (1694–1778)

• • • • • • • • • • • • • • •

The Different Names of Father Christmas Around the World

Papai Noel – Brazil

Viejo Pascuero ('Old Man Christmas') – Chile

Dun Che Lao Ren ('Christmas Old Man'), or Shengdan Laoren – China

St Nicholas – Europe

Joulupukki – Finland

Père Noël – France

**Weihnachtsmann ('Christmas Man')
or St Nikolaus – Germany**

Kanakaloka – Hawaii

**Tel-apo/Mikulás/ Winter
Grandfather – Hungary**

Santa Claus, Baba – India

Babbo Natale – Italy

**Hoteiosho (a god or priest who
brings gifts) – Japan**

Kaled Senelis – Lithuania

Black Peter – Morocco

**De Kerstman or Sinterklaas –
The Netherlands**

**Julenissen ('Christmas gnome') –
Norway**

Papa Noel – Peru

Swiety Mikolaj (St Nicholas) – Poland

Ded Moroz ('Grandfather Frost') – Russia

Tomten/Jultomten ('Christmas brownie') – Sweden

Father Christmas – UK

Santa Claus – USA, Canada

Part 3:

THINGS

1. SCIENCE AND THE NATURAL WORLD

●　●　●　●　●　●　●　●　●　●　●　●　●　●

The First Dinosaurs to Be Named (and Their Meanings)

The first 10 dinosaurs were all identified and named within a quarter of a century – although subsequent research has since cast doubt on the authenticity of certain specimens. After the 1850s, the hunting, identifying and naming of dinosaurs became highly competitive, with dinosaurologists vying with each other to discover and assign names to every new find.

1. Megalosaurus – 'Great Lizard'

The name Megalosaurus was proposed by William Buckland (1784–1856), an English geologist and noted eccentric (out of scientific curiosity he ate the mummified heart of the French king, Louis XIV). The name had actually been suggested to him by another clergyman-geologist, the Rev. William Daniel Conybeare, but Buckland was the first to use it in an article, 'Notice on the Megalosaurus or Great Fossil Lizard of Stonesfield', which was published in 1824.

2. Iguanodon – 'Iguana Tooth'
3. Hylaeosaurus – 'Woodland Lizard'

Both discovered by Gideon Algernon Mantell (1790–1852), a doctor from Sussex who devoted much of his life to studying geology. Mantell (or, according to some, his wife Mary Ann) found the first Iguanodon teeth in 1822 in a pile of stones being used for road repairs in the Tilgate Forest area of Sussex. He thought they resembled enormous iguana teeth, and suggested the name Iguanodon. In 1833 he was to assign the name Hylaeosaurus to another of his finds.

4. Macrodontophion – 'Long-toothed Snake'

Named by Polish nobleman A. Zborzewski in 1836.

5. Palaeosaurus – 'Ancient Lizard'
6. Thecodontosaurus – 'Socket-toothed Lizard'

Named by British geologists Samuel Stutchbury and Henry Riley in 1836.

7. Palateosaurus – 'Flat Lizard'

Named by German palaeontologist Hermann von Meyer in 1837.

8. Poekilopleuron – 'Varying Side'

Named by Jacques Armand Eudes-Deslongchamps in 1838.

9. Cietosaurus – 'Whale Lizard'
10. Cladeiodon – 'Branch Tooth'

Named in 1841 by Richard Owen, who first coined the word 'Dinosauria' – 'fearfully great lizards' – and was the driving force behind the creation in 1854 of the life-sized dinosaur models at Crystal Palace, London, which can be seen to this day.

Lakes Named After People

Lake Victoria, Uganda/Kenya/Tanzania

Queen Victoria (1819–1901), British monarch

Lake Albert, Uganda/Democratic Republic of Congo

Prince Albert (1819–61), Queen Victoria's husband

Lake Edward, Uganda/Democratic Republic of Congo

Edward VII (1841–1910), British monarch

Lake Nasser, Egypt

Gamal Nasser (1918–70), president of Egypt

General Carrera Lake, Argentina/Chile

José Miguel Carrera (1785–1821), Chilean general

Lake Champlain, Canada/USA

Samuel de Champlain (1567–1635), French navigator

O'Higgins/San Martín Lake, Chile/Argentina

José de San Martín (1778–1850) and Bernado O'Higgins (1778–1842), Chilean independence fighters

Lake Amadeus, Australia

King Amadeus of Spain (1845–90)

Lac Saint-Jean, Quebec, Canada

Jean de Quen (1603–59), French Jesuit missionary

Lake Mead, Nevada, USA
Elwood Mead (1858–1936), American engineer

Chemical Elements Named After People and Places

Chemical elements are the building blocks of nature, and scientists have spent a lot of time trying to identify them. It is customary for the scientist who discovers the element to decide on its name. Sometimes they name them after themselves – and sometimes they get a little more creative!

Each element has an official name, a shortened chemical symbol, and an atomic number, which indicates the number of protons in the nucleus of each atom of the element.

Americium (Am/95)
America

Berkelium (Bk/97)
Berkeley, California

Bohrium (Bh/107)
Danish physicist Niels Bohr (1885–1962)

Californium (Cf/98)
California and University of California, Berkeley

Cerium (Ce/58)
Ceres, Roman goddess of agriculture

Copernicium (Cn/112)
Renaissance astronomer Nicolaus Copernicus (1473–1543)

Copper (Cu/29)
Probably named after Cyprus, where it was
mined during the Roman era

Curium (Cm/96)
Pierre (1859–1906) and Marie Curie (1867–1934), the French/
Polish physicists who themselves discovered radium

Darmstadtium (Ds/110)
Darmstadt, Germany

Dubnium (Db/105)
Dubna, Russia

Einsteinium (Es/99)
German physicist Albert Einstein (1879–1955)

Europium (Eu/63)
The continent of Europe

Fermium (Fm/100)
Italian-American physicist Enrico Fermi (1901–54)

Francium (Fr/87)
Francia – Latin for France

Gadolinium (Gd/64)
Finnish scientist Johan Gadolin (1760–1852)

Gallium (Ga/31)
Gallia – Latin for Gaul or France

Germanium (Ge/32)
Germania – Latin for Germany

Hafnium (Hf/72)
Hafnia – Latin for Copenhagen

Hassium (Hs/108)
Hassia – Latin for Hesse in Germany

Helium (He/2)
Helios – the Greek name for the Sun

Holmium (Ho/67)
Holmia – Latin for Stockholm

Iridium (Ir/77)
Iris, from Greek mythology

Lutetium (Lu/71)
Lutetia – Latin for Paris

Magnesium (Mg/12)
Magnesia, a region of Greece

Mendelevium (Md/101)
Russian chemist Dmitri Mendeleyev (1834–1907)

Niobium (Nb/41)
Niobe, a mortal woman in Greek mythology

Nobelium (No/102)
Alfred Nobel, inventor of dynamite and
founder of the Nobel Prizes (1833–96)

Palladium (Pd/46)
The asteroid Pallas, named after the goddess Pallas Athene

Polonium (Po/84)
Polonia – Latin for Poland

Promethium (Pm/61)
Prometheus, a Titan from Greek mythology

Röntgenium (Rg/111)
German physicist Wilhelm Röntgen (1845–1923)

Rutherfordium (Rf/104)
British scientist Ernest Rutherford (1871–1937)

Scandium (Sc/21)
Scandia – Latin for Scandinavia

Seaborgium (Sg/106)
Glenn T. Seaborg, American scientist (1912–99)

Selenium (Se/34)
Selene, the Greek name for the Moon

Tantalum (Ta/73)
Tantalus, from Greek mythology

Tellurium (Te/52)
Tellus – the Latin name for the Earth

Thorium (Th/90)
Thor, the Norse god of thunder

Thulium (Tm/69)
Thule, a mythical island in the far north, perhaps Scandinavia

Titanium (Ti/22)
The Titans, from Greek mythology

Vanadium (V/23)
Vanadis, Scandinavian goddess of beauty

Weighty People
Men and Women Who Had Measurements Named After Them

Ampere
Electrical current, André-Marie Ampère (French, 1775–1836)

Angstrom
Light, Anders Jonas Ångstrom (Swedish, 1814–74)

Apgar score
Baby health, Virginia Apgar (US, 1909–74)

Beaufort scale
Wind speed, Sir Francis Beaufort (British, 1774–1857

Becquerel
Radioactivity, Henri Becquerel (French, 1852–1908)

Bel/decibel
Sound, Alexander Graham Bell (Scots/US, 1847–1922)

Binet-Simon scale
Intelligence, Alfred Binet (French, 1857–1911);
Théodore Simon (French, 1873–1964)

Celsius

Temperature, Anders Celsius (Swedish, 1701–44)

Coriolis force

Rotation, Gaspard Gustave de Coriolis (French, 1792–1843)

Coulomb

Electrical charge, Charles Augustus de Coulomb
(French, 1736–1806)

Curie

Radiation, Marie Curie (Polish/French, 1867–1934)

Dobson unit

Ozone layer, Gordon Miller Bourne Dobson
(British, 1889–1976)

Einstein unit

Electromagnetic energy, Albert Einstein
(German/US, 1879–1955)

Eotvos unit

Gravity, Baron Roland von Eotvos (Hungarian, 1848–1919)

Fahrenheit

Temperature, Gabriel Fahrenheit (German, 1686–1736)

Farad

Electrical capacitance, Michael Faraday (British, 1791–1867)

Gauss

Magnetic field, Karl Friedrich Gauss (German, 1777–1855)

Henry

Electrical inductance, Joseph Henry (US, 1797–1878)

Hertz
Frequency, Heinrich Rudolf Hertz (German, 1857–94)

Joule
Energy, James Prescott Joule (British, 1818–89)

Kelvin
Temperature, William Thomson,
Lord Kelvin (British, 1824–1907)

Mach number
Speed of sound, Ernst Mach (Austrian, 1838–1916)

Maxwell
Magnetism, James Clerk Maxwell (British, 1831–79)

Mercalli scale
Earthquakes, Giuseppe Mercalli (Italian, 1850–1914)

Mohs scale
Hardness, Friedrich Mohs (German, 1773–1839)

Newton
Force, Sir Isaac Newton (British, 1642–1727)

Ohm/Mho
Electrical resistance, Georg Simon Ohm (German, 1787–1854)
(a 'Mho' is a reciprocal 'Ohm')

Pascal
Pressure, Blaise Pascal (French, 1623–62)

Planck
Energy, Max Karl Ernst Ludwig Planck (German, 1858–1947)

Réaumur
Temperature, René Antoine Ferchault de Réaumur (French, 1683–1757)

Reynolds number
Fluid flow, Osborne Reynolds (British, 1842–1912)

Richter scale
Earthquakes, Charles Richter (US, 1900–85)

Röntgen
Radiation, Wilhelm Konrad Röntgen (German, 1845–1923)

Siemens
Conductivity, Karl Wilhelm Siemens (German/British, 1822–83)

Stanton number
Fluid convection, Thomas Stanton (British, 1865–1931)

Strouhal number
Sound, Vincenc Strouhal (Czech, 1850–1922)

Tesla
Magnetic induction, Nikola Tesla (Croatian/US, 1856–1943)

Volt
Electromagnetic force, Alessandro Volta (Italian, 1745–1827)

Watt
Power, James Watt (British, 1736–1819)

Weber
Magnetic flux, Wilhelm Eduard Weber (German, 1804–91)

Wechsler test
Intelligence, David Wechsler (US, 1896–1981)

Young's modulus
Elasticity, Thomas Young (British, 1773–1829)

Hurricanes

Hurricanes are given people's names to help distinguish them
and make them easier to refer to in conversation.
These names are decided in advance and assigned
by the World Meteorlogical Association in alphabetical
order as hurricanes appear. So for 2012 the
North Atlantic hurricanes will be called:

Alberto
Beryl
Chris
Debby
Ernesto
Florence
Gordon
Helene
Isaac
Joyce
Kirk
Leslie
Michael
Nadine

Oscar
Patty
Rafael
Sandy
Tony
Valerie
William

If these names are exhausted by the end of the year, they move
on to Greek letters (Alpha, Beta, Gamma, etc.) instead.

Retired Hurricanes

Hurricane names are normally re-used, but occasionally a
hurricane causes so much damage or loss of life that its name
is retired from use. Here are a few of the deadliest or most
damaging storms ever to have been retired.

Hurricane Hugo

In 1989 hurricane Hugo hit Guadaloupe and continued north
as far as South Carolina. It caused 56 fatalities, and over $10
billion of damage, making it the most damaging hurricane
recorded at that time.

Hurricane Katrina

This 2005 hurricane was both deadly and costly, causing
1,836 confirmed deaths and over $81 billion worth of damage.
The most damage was done to the city of New Orleans, with
80% of the city becoming flooded.

Hurricane Mitch

In 1998 this storm reached speeds of 180 mph over
Central America, but it was the huge amount of rainfall

and the resultant flooding that caused the official
death toll to reach 19,325.

Hurricane Pauline

This Pacific hurricane landed in Mexico in 1997 and was
considerably less deadly than Mitch, directly causing between
230 and 400 deaths. However, it did cause an estimated $7.5
billion of damage, and destroyed tens of thousands of homes.

Hurricane Stan

Another 2005 storm that was relatively weak and only briefly
reached hurricane status, yet still contributed to 1,628 deaths
in Mexico as a result of flooding and mudslides.

The Names of the Months

January

Named after Janus, the god of doors and gates

February

Named after Februalia, a time period when sacrifices
were made to atone for sins

March

Named after Mars, the god of war

April

From *aperire*, Latin for 'to open' (buds)

May

Named after Maia, the goddess of growth of plants

June

From Junius, Latin for 'of [the goddess] Juno'

July
Named after Julius Caesar in 44 BC

August
Named after Augustus Caesar in 8 BC

September
From *septem*, Latin for 'seven'

October
From *octo*, Latin for 'eight'

November
From *novem*, Latin for 'nine'

December
From *decem*, Latin for 'ten'

NOTE: The earliest Latin calendar was a 10-month one, beginning with March; thus, September was the seventh month, October, the eighth, etc. July was originally called *Quintilis*, meaning fifth; August was originally called *Sextilis*, meaning sixth.

Renaming the Months

In 1793, after the French Revolution, France adopted a new calendar with 10 days in each week and 12 months of 30 days each, with names relating to the seasons. It began in late September with the autumn equinox.

Vendémiaire ('grape harvest')
Brumaire ('fog')
Frimaire ('frost')

Nivôse ('snowy')
Pluviôse ('rainy')
Ventôse ('windy')
Germinal ('germination')
Floréal ('flower')
Prairial ('pasture')
Messidor ('harvest')
Thermidor ('summer heat')
Fructidor ('fruit')

It was unpopular and was abandoned in 1805.

Animals Named After People

In the study of zoology, animals have two names – a common name, such as 'dog', 'mouse' or 'tiger', and also a scientific name. The scientific name has two parts, the first referring to the genus that the creature belongs to, and the second referring to its species. For example, the common house cat is known as 'felis catus' – *felis* being the genus, and *catus* being the species.

The scientific names are also known as Latin names, as it is common to Latinize the names of other people or things in order to create a new species name. Below are some species that have been given Latinized names of famous people.

Aegrotocatellus jaggeri
(Trilobite)
Mick Jagger (1943–), musician with The Rolling Stones

Agathidium bushi
(Slime mould beetle)
George W. Bush (1946–), 43rd president of the USA

Agathidium vaderi
(Fungus beetle)
Darth Vader, character from *Star Wars,* who has a similar black, helmet-like head

Agra katewinsletae
(Ground beetle)
Kate Winslet (1975–), actress

Agra schwarzeneggeri
(Carabid)
Arnold Schwarzenegger (1947–),
Terminator actor and politician

Albunea groeningi
(Sand crab)
Matt Groening (1954–), creator of *The Simpsons*

Anhanguera spielbergi
(Pterosaur)
Steven Spielberg (1946–), director of *E.T.,
Jurassic Park* and *Indiana Jones*

Anophthalmus hitleri
(Blind cave beetle)
Adolf Hitler (1889–1945), German dictator

Aptostichus angelinajolieae
(Trapdoor spider)
Angelina Jolie (1975–), actress

Arthurdactylus conandoylei
(Pterosaur)
Arthur Conan Doyle (1859–1930), author of *The Lost World*,
a book that featured pterosaurs

Avahi cleesei
(Woolly lemur)
John Cleese (1939–), comedian who has
worked to protect lemurs in the wild

Avalanchurus simoni
(Trilobite)
Paul Simon (1941–), singer-songwriter

Avalanchurus lennoni
(Trilobite)
John Lennon (1940–80), musician with The Beatles

Avalanchurus starri
(Trilobite)
Ringo Starr (1940–), drummer with The Beatles

Baeturia hardyi
(Cicada)
Oliver Hardy (1892–1957), comic actor

Baeturia laureli
(Cicada)
Stan Laurel (1890–1965), comic actor

Bishopina mozarti
(Ostracod)
Wolfgang Amadeus Mozart (1756–91), composer

Bufonaria borisbeckeri
(Sea snail)
Boris Becker (1967–), tennis champion

Caloplaca Obamae
(Lichen)
Barack Obama (1961–), 44th president of the USA

Campsicnemius charliechaplini
(Fly)
Charlie Chaplin (1889–1977), comic silent movie actor

Cirolana mercuryi
(Isopod)
Freddie Mercury (1946–91), singer with the band Queen

Draculoides bramstokeri
(Troglobite)
Bram Stoker (1847–1912), author of *Dracula*; this arachnid has large fangs like the famous vampire

Eristalis gatesi
(Flower fly)
Bill Gates (1955–), founder of Microsoft

Hyla stingi
(Colombian tree frog)
Sting (1951–), musician and environmentalist

Legionella shakespearei
(Bacterium)
William Shakespeare (1564–1616), playwright

Marxella
(Wasp)
Karl Marx (1818–83), German philosopher

Myrmekiaphila neilyoungi
(Trapdoor spider)
Neil Young (1945–), singer-songwriter

Norasaphus monroeae
(Trilobite)
Marilyn Monroe (1926–62), actress; the trilobite has an hourglass shape reminiscent of the actress

Orontobia dalailama
(Tiger moth)
Dalai Lama (1935–), Tibetan religious leader

Pachygnatha zappa
(Orb-weaver spider)
Frank Zappa (1940–93), musician whose moustache resembles
the markings on the spider!

Perirehaedulus richardsi
(Trilobite)
Keith Richards (1943–), musician with The Rolling Stones

Pheidole harrisonfordi
(Ant)
Harrison Ford (1942–), *Star Wars* and *Indiana Jones* actor

Preseucoila imallshookupis
(Gall wasp)
Elvis Presley (1935–77), musician, and his
song 'I'm All Shook Up'

Psephophorus terrypratchetti
(Turtle)
Terry Pratchett (1948–), author of the Discworld® novels,
which are set on the back of a giant turtle

Serendipaceratops arthurcclarkei
(Ornithischia dinosaur)
Arthur C. Clarke (1917–2008), science-fiction author

Serratoterga garylarsoni
(Butterfly)
US cartoonist Gary Larson (1950–)

Stasimopus mandelai
(Sea slug)
Nelson Mandela (1918–), South African leader

Struszia mccartneyi
(Trilobite)
Paul McCartney (1942–), musician with The Beatles

And a Few Animals with Common Names That Come from Real People . . .

Dobermann pinscher
Karl Friedrich Louis Dobermann, who bred the dogs

Guppy
John Robert Lechmere Guppy (1836–1916),
who first discovered these fish in Trinidad

Jack Russell

Reverend John Russell (1795–1883), who bred the dogs

Père David's deer

Armand David (1826–1900), who made the species known to the Western world

Przewalski's horse

Nikolai Przhevalsky (1839–88), Russian explorer and first known European to describe the species

St Bernard dog

Bernard of Menthon (923–1008), who named the St Bernard Pass in the Alps where the dogs were first recorded

Wilson's Storm Petrel

Alexander Wilson (1766–1813), Scottish ornithologist

Celebrity Animals

Sometimes the animals themselves are more famous than the people they are named for! These are all real animals that went on to become famous.

Athena

The pet owl that nurse Florence Nightingale acquired in Athens, Greece, died in 1855 and is preserved at the Florence Nightingale Museum in St Thomas's Hospital, London.

Brumas the polar bear

Brumas, who was born in 1949, was the first polar bear to be successfully reared in the UK. She was so popular with visitors to London Zoo that their annual attendance figures trebled. Her name was created by mixing the names of two of her zookeepers – the first three letters of 'Bruce' added to 'Sam' spelled backwards.

Chi Chi

The giant panda Chi Chi was one of the most popular animals at London Zoo, where she lived from 5 September 1958 to 22 July 1972. Her body, stuffed by taxidermist Roy Hale, has since been displayed at the Natural History Museum. The WWF panda symbol was based on drawings of Chi Chi by naturalist Gerald Watterson.

Dolly

Dolly the sheep, the world's first cloned mammal, was born on 5 July 1996 at the Roslin Institute, Edinburgh, and named after the Country & Western singer Dolly Parton. Since Dolly's death on 14 February 2002, her body has been exhibited by the Royal Museum of Scotland.

Eclipse

The racehorse Eclipse took his name from a solar eclipse at the time of his birth, 1 April 1764. He won every race by such a huge margin that other owners refused to race their horses against him. He retired to stud (as many as 95% of today's thoroughbreds are thought to contain Eclipse DNA) and died in 1789. In an attempt to discover the secret of his speed, his body was studied, laying the foundations for veterinary medicine in Britain. His skeleton is displayed at the Royal Veterinary College, Hawkshead, Hertfordshire.

Goldie the golden eagle

Goldie the golden eagle escaped from London Zoo in 1965, and the entire country became glued to news reports of his flights over Regent's Park. He evaded recapture by the zookeepers for 12 days before being brought back to the zoo, though not for long – he escaped again in December of the same year!

Guy the gorilla

Guy arrived at London Zoo on Guy Fawkes Day 1947, hence his name. He died there on 8 June 1978 and was stuffed by taxidermist Arthur Hayward at the Natural History Museum, where he remains.

Jumbo the elephant

Surprisingly, Jumbo the elephant was not named for his size – the word 'jumbo', meaning 'large', actually derives from the elephant himself! He was a popular exhibit at London Zoo in the late 19th century – so much so that when renowned circus owner P. T. Barnum bought him, 100,000 school children wrote to Queen Victoria asking her not to sell!

London Jack

From 1894 to 1900 a dog called London Jack carried a box at Paddington Station, London – one of several that collected money for the families of railwaymen killed at work. After his death, Jack's body was preserved and displayed in a glass case until 1921. It is now in the Natural History Museum, Tring, Hertfordshire, with over 80 other notable dogs.

Mia the cobra

This as-yet-unnamed cobra escaped from the reptile exhibit at the Bronx Zoo, New York, USA, in early 2011, and was missing for six days before being found. She was named Mia in an online poll as an acronym of Missing In Action.

Mick the Miller

Considered greyhound racing's greatest champion, in his

brief career (1929–31), Mick the Miller won five classic races and was the first dog to win the English Derby twice. After his death in 1939, Mick was mounted and displayed at the Natural History Museum, London, before being transferred to Tring.

Obaysch

Obaysch was named after the island on which he was captured, and as the first hippopotamus to come to Britain since prehistoric times, he was sensationally popular.

Pipaluk the polar bear

Pipaluk was another male polar bear raised at London Zoo after Brumas. His name comes from the Inuit (Eskimo) word for 'the little one'.

Fictional Animal Names

These animals might not really exist in nature, but we love them anyway! Here are some notable animals from the worlds of fiction.

Aslan, the lion from *The Chronicles of Narnia* by C. S. Lewis

Aslan the talking lion first appeared in *The Lion, the Witch and the Wardrobe*, and is a heroic figure who guides the children on their adventures in Narnia. His name comes from the Turkish for 'lion'.

Bugs Bunny, from the Warner Bros cartoons and films

This animated rabbit was originally created without a name, but was accidentally given the nickname of one of his creators,

Ben 'Bugs' Hardaway. Without knowing what to call it, one of the early cartoon's animators wrote 'Bugs's Bunny' on a model sheet (meaning 'the rabbit created by Bugs') and the name stuck.

Donkey Kong, the ape from the Nintendo video-game series

This video-game character has nothing to do with donkeys; his name comes from his designer's mistaken belief that the word 'donkey' meant 'stupid' in English. The 'Kong' part was chosen for its link to apes, so the name was meant to suggest 'stupid ape'. Entertainment company MCA Universal attempted to sue Nintendo, believing that the character was a rip-off of King Kong from the popular movies, but the claim was dismissed.

Garfield, a cat from the Jim Davis comic strip

Garfield is an overweight orange tabby cat who loves lasagne and hates Mondays. His creator named him after his own grandfather, James Garfield Davis, and his grandfather was in turn named after former US president James A. Garfield.

Hedwig, the snowy owl from the *Harry Potter* series by J. K. Rowling

Hedwig is a snowy owl who acts as a messenger for the boy wizard Harry Potter, often helping him to communicate when no other means are possible. Writer J. K. Rowling claims to have found the name in a book of medieval saints (possibly St Hedwig of Andechs, 1174–1243), and this is reflected in the books when Harry gives his own owl a name he discovers in his school book *A History of Magic*.

Jumble, a dog from Richmal Crompton's *Just William* stories

William Brown's scruffy mongrel dog appears in the very first William book, and it is explained in the story 'Jumble' that he was given to William as a reward for posing for a prize-winning painting. He was played by a dog called Iva in the 2010 CBBC series.

Mickey Mouse, from the Disney cartoons

Mickey Mouse was created by Walt Disney as a replacement for Oswald the Lucky Rabbit, after contract negotiations meant Disney was unable to continue making Oswald cartoons. The character was at one early stage called Mortimer Mouse before being renamed Mickey. American actor Mickey Rooney once claimed that he met Disney during the design of the character, and that the mouse was named after him, but this has not been confirmed.

Napoleon, a pig from *Animal Farm* by George Orwell

Napolean is a pig in this story of a group of animals who take over a farm. Initially they work together, but Napoleon gradually takes over and turns the farm into a dictatorship. Orwell wrote the book as an allegory of the Russian Revolution, and Napoleon was intended to represent tyrannical leader Joseph Stalin. However, the name comes from another dictator – French general Napoleon Bonaparte. In the French edition the character was called César after Roman statesman Julius Caesar.

Nemo, a clownfish from the movie *Finding Nemo*

Nemo, the clownfish who goes missing at the start of this Pixar film, was named after the character of Captain Nemo in Jules Verne's book *20,000 Leagues Under the Sea*. Interestingly, Verne got the name from the Latin for 'no one', so the film title actually means 'finding no one'!

Paddington Bear, from the stories by Michael Bond

Michael Bond was inspired to create the character after buying his wife a toy bear from a shop near Paddington Station. Originally appearing in the book *A Bear Called Paddington*, Paddington Brown is named after being found by the Brown family on Paddington Station with a note that reads *Please look after this bear. Thank you.*

Scrooge McDuck, from the Disney comics and cartoons

Scrooge is Donald Duck's uncle, and he takes his first name from Ebenezer Scrooge – a similarly miserly character from Charles Dickens's *A Christmas Carol*. The surname is intended to suggest his Scottish roots, and there is a theory that the character was partly inspired by Scottish industrialist Andrew Carnegie.

Shadowfax, Gandalf the White's horse from *The Lord of the Rings* by J. R. R. Tolkien

Shadowfax is given to the wizard Gandalf by King Théoden of Rohan, and it is said that he carries Gandalf from his own choice and can gallop faster than any horse in

Middle-earth. His name means 'shadow-mane' and comes from the old Norse word 'fax' for mane. Other horses in Norse mythology are named in a similar fashion – Skinfaki (shining mane) and Hrímfaxi (frost mane).

Snowball II from *The Simpsons*

Snowball II is a cat belonging to the Simpsons in the animated sitcom. Unlike a lot of cartoon animals she generally acts like a real cat, and cannot speak. The Simpson's first cat, Snowball I, was named for its white fur, which makes the naming of the black Snowball II somewhat ironic.

Sonic the Hedgehog from the Sega video-game series

Sonic was created as a new mascot for the Sega company in the early 1990s. Named for his supersonic speed as he runs and jumps his way through his games, he was at one point in the game's development called 'Mr Needlemouse'.

Winnie-the-Pooh, the bear from the books by A. A. Milne

This honey-loving bear who lives in the Hundred Acre Wood has starred in many books and films. Milne based the character on a teddy bear owned by his son, Christopher, who in turn named the bear after two animals – Winnie, a Canadian black bear in London Zoo, and Pooh, a swan who lived on a lake near the Milne family's cottage.

Fictional Robot and Computer Names

Science still has a way to go before we see robots and computers as advanced as some of these! Although mechanical humans have featured in stories for hundreds of years, the word 'robot' was invented in 1921 by Czech writer Karel Capek in his play RUR (Rossum's Universal Robots). Since then, robots have appeared in many books, films and TV programmes. These are some of the best known:

B.E.N. (Bio-Electronic Navigator)

A robot who is suffering from memory loss in the 2002 animated film *Treasure Planet*.

Bender (full name: Bender Bending Rodriguez)

The robot in the Futurama animated series (1999–2003). In the show, he is designed by Mom's Friendly Robot Company for the purpose of bending girders, but he actually spends his time working as a delivery bot for Planet Express, and talking of his desire to 'kill all humans'.

C-3PO & R2-D2

These two robot friends are the first characters we meet in the original *Star Wars* film (1977), and are the only two characters in the film series to appear in all six films being portrayed by the same two actors.

Daleks and Cybermen

Doctor Who's two most formidable enemies are actually cyborgs rather than robots, in that they have both biological and mechanical parts. The Daleks were created by Terry

Nation in 1963 for the second *Doctor Who* serial, and they caused an immediate sensation all over the UK. The Cybermen first appeared in the 1966 story *The Tenth Planet*, and both races have gone up against the Doctor many times since.

D.A.R.Y.L.

From a 1985 film of the same name. His name comes from 'Data Analyzing Robot Youth Lifeform', and in the story he is designed by the government as an experiment in artificial intelligence.

David

The android in the film *A.I. Artificial Intelligence* (2001) – originally from the Brian Aldiss short story *Super-Toys Last All Summer Long* (1969). This android looks human, and is programmed with the ability to love.

Deep Thought

The supercomputer programmed to calculate the ultimate answer to life, the universe and everything in Douglas Adams's *The Hitchhiker's Guide to the Galaxy* and its sequels (1979–92) and film (2005).

HAL 9000

A sentient computer onboard the Discovery One spacecraft in Arthur C. Clarke's *Space Odyssey* saga, including the film *2001: A Space Odyssey* (1968). The name stands for Heuristically programmed ALgorithmic computer.

The Iron Man

The giant robot who arrives from an unknown place in Ted Hughes's children's story of the same name (1968) and the film (1999). In America the name was changed to *The Iron Giant* to avoid confusion with the Marvel Comics character Iron Man.

K-9

From *Doctor Who*, *The Sarah Jane Adventures*, and also his own show K-9. He is called K-9 because it sounds like the word 'canine', which means 'dog-like'. He was followed by K-9 MkII and K-9 MkIII.

Marvin the Paranoid Android

The depressed robot who is constantly suffering from pain in all the diodes down his left side in Douglas Adams's The *Hitchhiker's Guide to the Galaxy* radio series (1978–2005), novel series (1979–1992, with a sixth written by Eoin Colfer in 2009), and film adaptation (2005).

The Mechadrones, the Galvanic Mechomorphs, Ship, Slix Vigma and S.A.M.

All robots that appear in the *Ben 10* cartoon series (2005–).

Mr Smith

The extraterrestrial supercomputer that aids Sarah-Jane Smith and her friends in *The Sarah-Jane Adventure*s. It is actually from a race of creatures called the Xylok.

Optimus Prime, leader of the Autobots, and Megatron, leader of the Decepticons

The leaders of the two warring factions in *Transformers* (2007) and its sequels *Transformers: Revenge of the Fallen* (2009) and *Transformers: Dark of the Moon* (2011). They were originally created as toys in 1984.

Robby the Robot

The robot in the classic science-fiction film *Forbidden Planet* (1956), which later gave its name to two separate chains of science-fiction, fantasy and horror bookshops in the UK and the US.

T-800

The almost indestructible time-travelling robot in the *Terminator* films (1984 and 1991). An upgraded model, the T-1000, appeared in *Terminator 2*, and the T–850 and T-X Terminatrix appeared in *Terminator 3* (2003).

Tik-Tok

A clockwork robot in Frank Baum's book *Ozma of Oz* (1907) and 1985 film *Return to Oz*.

Wall-E and Eve

Two robots who fall in love from the Pixar movie *Wall-E* (2008). Wall-E is a robot programmed to clean up the rubbish on an abandoned planet Earth when Eve appears unexpectedly from a spaceship.

2. PETS

Top Cats' Names in the UK

1. Molly
2. Felix
3. Smudge
4. Sooty
5. Tigger
6. Charlie
7. Alfie
8. Oscar
9. Millie
10. Misty

The first cat recorded as having a name was Nedjem *(star)*, which comes from records of the reign of Egyptian pharaoh Thutmose III (1479–1425 BC).

Famous Cat-lovers and Their Cats' Names

Winston Churchill & Margate

The cat turned up at 10 Downing Street and was adopted by Churchill on 10 October 1953, the day of an important speech at Margate, hence its name. Later cat occupants of Number 10 have included Harold Wilson's Siamese cat Nemo, Margaret

Thatcher's Wilberforce, Humphrey, a stray who moved in during Mrs Thatcher's residence and stayed into the periods of office of John Major and Tony Blair, and Larry, adopted from the Battersea Dogs and Cats Home by David Cameron to tackle Number 10's rat problem!

Charles Dickens & Williamina

Williamina was called William until she gave birth to a litter of kittens, one of which, known as 'the Master's Cat', gained Dickens's attention by putting out his candle with its paw.

T. S. Eliot & George Pushdragon, Tantomile, etc.

The noted author of *Old Possum's Book of Practical Cats* (1939), which became the long-running musical *Cats*, owned numerous cats.

Edward Lear & Foss

Foss was the subject of a number of Lear's nonsense poems and comic drawings. When the cat died in 1887, Lear claimed he was 31 years old.

President Abraham Lincoln & Tabby

Cared for by US president Lincoln's son Tad, Tabby was an early example of what became a White House cat tradition, continued in recent times with John F. Kennedy's Tom Kitten, Ronald Reagan's Cleo and Sara, Bill Clinton's Socks (whose 'Diary' became a bestselling book) and George W. Bush's India.

Domenico Scarlatti & Pulcinella

The Italian composer's cat used to jump onto his harpsichord
keyboard and stroll along the keys, inspiring
Scarlatti to compose 'The Cat's Fugue'.

Mark Twain & Tammany

Tammany was one of many cats belonging to
American writer Mark Twain, who described how one
of Tammany's kittens liked to sit in the pocket of his billiard
table watching games in progress.

Queen Victoria & White Heather

A Buckingham Palace resident, White Heather
outlived her mistress and thus became official court
cat to her son, King Edward VII.

Top Dogs' Names in the UK

1. Max
2. Molly
3. Sam/Sammy
4. Meg/Megan
5. Ben
6. Holly
7. Charlie
8. Oscar
9. Barney
10. Millie/Milly

Famous Dog-lovers and Their Dogs' Names

Francis Barraud & Nipper

British artist Francis Barraud created a painting entitled His Master's Voice, which showed his dog Nipper listening to a gramophone. The image was later used as the logo for HMV.

J. M. Barrie & Luath

Luath was a Newfoundland dog who belonged to writer J. M. Barrie, and the model for Nana in his book *Peter Pan*.

President George H. W. Bush & Millie

The US president's springer spaniel Millie had her bestselling 'autobiography' *Millie's Book* written by First Lady Barbara Bush.

Lord Byron & Boatswain

When this poet's dog died of rabies, Byron wrote a poem called 'Epitaph to a Dog', which was inscribed onto Boatswain's tomb on Byron's estate Newstead Abbey. You can tell the dog was important to him, as the tomb is larger than Byron's own!

Lee Duncan & Rin Tin Tin

Rescued as a puppy from a German trench in France at the end of the First World War, the German shepherd Rin Tin Tin was taken to the USA, where he became famous as an animal film star.

President Barack Obama & Bo

A Portuguese water dog, given to his daughters, Malia and Sasha, as a reward after Obama's long campaign to become President.

Charles Schulz & Spike

American cartoonist Charles Schulz based his comic character Snoopy on his family's basset hound Spike. In later strips Spike himself appears as Snoopy's brother.

Queen Victoria & Dash

Dash, a King Charles spaniel, was Princess Victoria's dog when she became Queen in 1837.

Crufts' Best in Show Winners

Names like Max, Molly or Sam may be very popular, but dogs that compete at Crufts are given unique names to identify them. Here are some of the more oddly named winners at Crufts, along with the years in which they won. Imagine having to yell out some of these names in the park!

Abraxas Audacity

Bull Terrier (1972)

Araki Fabulous Willy

Tibetan Terrier (2007)

Bournehouse Dancing Master

English Setter (1977)

Bramshaw Bob

Labrador Retriever (1932, 1933)

Brookewire Brandy of Layven

Wire Fox Terrier (1975)

Burtonswood Bossyboots

Saint Bernard (1974)

Caitland Isle Take a Chance
Australian Shepherd (2006)

Caspians Intrepid
Irish Setter (1999)

Chiming Bells
Pointer (1958)

Cobyco Call the Tune
Whippet (2004)

Elch Elder of Ouborough
Great Dane (1953)

Exquisite Model of Ware
Cocker Spaniel (1938, 1939)

Fenton of Kentwood
Alsatian (1965)

Ginger Xmas Carol
Airedale Terrier (1986)

Grayco Hazelnut
Poodle (1982)

Harrowhill Huntsman
Wire Fox Terrier (1978)

Heather Necessity
Scottish Terrier (1929)

Hungargunn Bear It'n Mind
Hungarian Vizsla (2010)

Luckystar of Ware
Cocker Spaniel (1930, 1931)

Montravia Tommy-Gun
Standard Poodle (1985)

Noways Chuckles
Bulldog (1952)

Oakington Puckshill Amber Sunblush
Poodle (1966)

Olac Moon Pilot
West Highland White Terrier (1990)

Ozmilion Mystification
Yorkshire Terrier (1997)

Pencloe Dutch Gold
Whippet (1992)

Pennine Prima Donna
Pointer (1935)

Potterdale Classic of Moonhill
Bearded Collie (1989)

Purston Hit and Miss of Brocolitia
Welsh Terrier (1994)

Ramacon Swashbuckler
German Shepherd Dog (1971)

Sandstorm Saracen
Welsh Terrier (1959)

Saredon Forever Young
Welsh Terrier (1998)

Saxonsprings Hackensack
Lhasa Apso (1984)

Shargleam Blackcap
Retriever (Flat-coated) (1980)

Southball Moonstone
Greyhound (1934)

Starchelle Chicago Bear
Irish Setter (1995)

Starlite Express at Valsett
English Setter (1988)

Stingray of Derryabah
Lakeland Terrier (1967)

Topscore Contradiction
Standard Poodle (2002)

Torums Scarf Michael
Kerry Blue Terrier (2000)

Tracey Witch of Ware
Cocker Spaniel (1948, 1950)

Treetops Golden Falcon
Greyhound (1956)

Yakee a Dangerous Liaison
Pekingese (2003)

Top Celebrity Names Given to Pets in the UK

Based on a survey of dogs and cats treated at the
PDSA's 47 PetAid hospitals.

1. Tyson (Mike)
2. Harry (Potter or Prince)
3. Ozzy (Osbourne)
4. Robbie (Williams)
5. Rooney (Wayne)
6. Beckham (David)
7. Paris (Hilton)
8. Elvis (Presley)

9. Jessie (Wallace –
Kat Slater in EastEnders)
10. Britney (Spears)

● ● ● ● ● ● ● ● ● ● ● ● ● ● ● ● ● ●

3. FOOD, SHOPS AND EVERYDAY STUFF

Food Named After People

Apple Charlotte

Known as 'the king of cooks and the cook of kings', the French master chef Marie-Antoine Carême (1784–1833) served such distinguished patrons as Charles Talleyrand (a leading French statesman) and Tsar Alexander I of Russia. It was while he was employed by the Prince Regent (later King George IV) at Brighton Pavilion (1816–19) that he created a new dessert, naming it Apple Charlotte after the prince's daughter.

Châteaubriand

Châteaubriand steak was named after François René, Vicomte de Châteaubriand (1768–1848), a Napoleonic statesman and notorious womanizer. In 1822 he was appointed Ambassador to Britain, and it was while he was living in London that his chef, Montmireil, perfected the method of cooking a piece of tender steak between two inferior pieces of meat, the juices of which it absorbed. He duly named it after his master.

Coquilles St Jacques

Coquille is French for shell – but why 'St Jacques'? Legend has it that the body of St James (Jacques in French) was being carried by sea from Joppa to Galicia in a miraculous ship without oars or sails. It sailed past the village of Bonzas in Portugal while a marriage ceremony was in progress, whereupon the bridegroom's horse rushed into the sea. The groom was saved from drowning by the saint's companions, and in gratitude converted to Christianity on the deck of the vessel. When he returned to the shore, his clothes were covered with scallop shells. The bridegroom converted the other villagers, who henceforth used the scallop shell as the symbol of St Jacques. Several centuries passed, however, before Coquilles St Jacques were embellished with Mornay sauce: this was invented by and named after Philippe de Mornay (1549–1623), a friend of Henry IV of France.

Eggs Arnold Bennett

Like the Pêche Melba, this omelette filled with haddock and cream originated at the Savoy Hotel in London. The writer and drama critic Arnold Bennett, whose novel Imperial Palace (1930) was based on the Savoy, often dined there after visiting the theatre. Too hungry to wait for a more elaborate meal, Eggs Arnold Bennett was created for him as an 'instant' dish.

Eggs Benedict

One morning in 1894, suffering from a hangover, Samuel Benedict, a New York man-about-town, entered the Waldorf-Astoria Hotel. He ordered the breakfast he habitually consumed as a cure-all – bacon, buttered toast, poached eggs and hollandaise sauce. On this occasion, however, Oscar, the maître d'hôtel, modified the dish, substituting ham and a muffin for the bacon and toast, christening the concoction Eggs Benedict in Samuel's honour. This is the traditional explanation, confirmed in later life by Oscar himself, but there is some evidence that the name may have come from another society figure, Mrs Le Grand Benedict.

Melba Toast

The great Australian opera singer Dame Nellie Melba
(1861–1931) had several dishes named after her, the most
famous of which is Pêche Melba. Toast Melba or Melba Toast
was also named for her, but was actually suggested by
Marie-Louise Ritz, wife of César Ritz, manager of the Savoy
Hotel in London. 'Toast is never thin enough to suit me,' she
remarked to Auguste Escoffier, head chef at the hotel. 'Can't
you do anything about it?' She suggested that he should try
toasting thin bread, then slicing it again and re-toasting it.
Escoffier retired to his kitchen, and his experiments resulted
in the dish he wanted to call 'Toast Marie' in honour of its
originator. However, Dame Nellie, exhausted from a strenuous
tour of America, was staying in the Savoy and was prescribed
a light diet while she recuperated. Escoffier duly served her his
newly created toast, which she adored. 'Call it Toast Melba,'
said the modest Marie Ritz, and Toast Melba it became.

Newburg Sauce

This popular seafood sauce is strangely called after
someone with a slightly different name, a 19th century
American shipping magnate called Charles Wenburg. It is said
that he discovered the recipe in South America and introduced
it to Delmonico's, his favourite New York restaurant, and as
'Lobster Wenburg' it was soon a regular feature of the menu.
On a subsequent visit to Delmonico's, Wenburg was allegedly
involved in a brawl and was thrown out. To crown his
ignominy, Lorenzo Delmonico, the restaurateur, punished
Wenburg by renaming the dish 'Lobster Newburg'.

Oysters Rockefeller

A dish created by billionaire John D. Rockefeller? Not exactly:
in 1899 Jules Alciatore of Antoine's Restaurant in New Orleans

devised this oyster dish; a customer declared it tasted 'as rich as Rockefeller' and so it acquired its opulent name.

Pavlova

The Pavlova, a meringue base topped with various fruits and cream, was named in honour of the great Russian ballerina Anna Pavlova (1885–1931) during a tour of Australia and New Zealand. In Australia its name is often shortened to 'Pav'.

Praline

César de Choiseul, Comte du Plessis-Praslin (1602–1675), was a precocious boy. Put in command of a regiment at the age of 14, he went on to achieve notoriety while still in his teens when he fought a duel in which not only he and his opponent were injured, but also both their seconds. He led the French army against Spain in 1650, and devoted his life to royal service – yet he is remembered less for his military achievements than for the fact that his chef prepared a sweet composed of sugar and almonds which became known as *praslin* – and ultimately as praline.

Sandwich

One of the most famous eponyms of all. John Montagu, 4th Earl of Sandwich (1718–92), is alleged to have had his servant put roast beef between slices of bread so that he could continue a marathon card game uninterrupted. Similar methods of eating were known at least as early as Roman times, but his name became irrevocably linked with this most familiar of foods – although his family attempted to rehabilitate his memory by insisting he invented 'sandwiches' because he was so busy with affairs of state.

Wimpy

The Popeye cartoon strip drawn by E. C. Segar (1894–1938) featured as one of its principal characters the gourmand J. Wellington Wimpy, whose main aim in life was apparently to eat as many hamburgers as he could cram into his mouth. The popularity of the cartoon was such that the name 'Wimpy' became both a synonym for a hamburger and a chain of hamburger restaurants. In addition, during the Second World War, the Wellington bomber was affectionately nicknamed the 'wimpy'.

Sweets and Snacks

Bourbon Biscuit

This chocolate cream sandwich biscuit is named after the House of Bourbon, a family of European monarchs.

Bourneville Bar

This dark chocolate bar from Cadbury's is named after a village that was founded by the chocolate manufacturers to house the workers at its factory in the West Midlands. The village itself was named after a local brook called 'Bourn Brook'.

Digestive Biscuit

Scottish inventor John Montgomerie filed a patent in 1889 which described the method of making these biscuits, and claimed that they would 'assist digestion, and be very light, agreeable, and nourishing food for people of weak digestion'. Today the biscuit makes no claims other than to taste nice with a cup of tea, but the name has remained.

Eccles Cake

A small round cake of pastry and currants that was first sold in a small shop in the English town of Eccles.

Garibaldi Biscuit

Made of currants squashed between two thin layers of biscuit, and named after Giuseppe Garibaldi (1807–82), an Italian military leader and national hero.

HobNob

The word 'hobnob', which today means 'to associate with in a friendly manner', first appears in Shakespeare's play *Twelfth Night*, and was chosen as a name for these oaty biscuits.

Jaffa Cake

A chocolate-covered sponge with a layer of orange-flavour jelly, this snack is named after Jaffa oranges, which were in turn named after the ancient city of Jaffa – part of modern-day Tel Aviv.

Kellogg's Corn Flakes

In 1894 the brothers Will Keith Kellogg (1830–1951) and Dr John Harvey Kellogg (1852–1943) were running their 'sanatorium', a health resort in Battle Creek, Michigan. Attempting to devise healthy food products for their patients, they experimented with wheat dough, which they boiled and passed through rollers. By accident, they discovered that if the dough was left overnight it came out as flakes, and that when these were baked they turned into a tasty cereal.
In 1898 they replaced wheat with corn, thereby creating the Corn Flakes we know today.

Kendal Mint Cake

A peppermint-flavoured glucose bar that was famously
used as a source of energy by Edmund Hillary and his team
during the first successful ascent of Mount Everest.
They are named for the town of Kendal in Cumbria,
England, where they were first manufactured.

Kit Kat

Even Nestlé, the makers of the Kit Kat, aren't completely
certain about the origins of this chocolate wafer bar's name.
The most likely (and rather long-winded!) story is that it
derives from a man called Christopher (Kit) Catlin, who lived
in London a good two centuries before the chocolate bar was
first manufactured. Kit Catlin owned a pie-house, and his
mutton pies became known as 'Kit-Kats'. A group of gentlemen
began to meet in this pie-house, and they formed a political
club which they named the Kit-Kat Club. This club later moved
to premises with a dining room that had a very low ceiling,
and so they needed shorter portraits than usual to hang on its
walls, and these became known in the art world as 'kit-cat portraits'. To make these portraits small enough to fit, they often
had to be snapped off at the top . . . in much the same way
you snap off a finger of a Kit Kat! It's quite an unusual
pie-maker who has a pie, a political club, a type of portrait,
and a chocolate bar named after him!

Lipton's Tea

Millionaire grocer Thomas Lipton originally set up a chain
of markets that lasted until the 1980s, but today he is
remembered for creating this brand of tea, as well as his rather
poor taste advertising: he once employed thin men to carry
signs that read GOING TO LIPTON'S and overweight men
to carry signs that read COMING FROM LIPTON'S!

He even offered Queen Victoria a five-ton cheese.
She refused, but knighted him anyway.

Maltesers

Chocolate-covered malt honeycomb balls.
The name is a blend of the words 'malt'
(one of its main ingredients) and 'teaser'.

Mars Bar

Chocolate bar with nougat and caramel, named for the
founder of the company, Franklin Clarence Mars.

Milky Way

A chocolate bar named after a popular malted milkshake
rather than the galaxy in which we live!

Polos

The mints with holes, supposedly linked to the
word 'polar' because of the cool and fresh
sensation you get from sucking one.

Quality Street

Chocolate selection boxes popular as gifts. The name comes
from the play *Quality Street* by J. M. Barrie. Two of the main
characters, the Major and Miss, appeared on the packaging
from its creation in 1936 until the year 2000.

Roses

A chocolate selection box made by Cadbury's and named after
the Rose brothers, who designed the machine used for packing
the individual chocolates.

Schweppes Soft Drinks

German-born Jean Jacob Schweppe (1740–1821) developed

the first practical way of manufacturing fizzy drinks. He moved to London in 1792 and began producing his own brand of soda water, forming Schweppe & Co. (later Schweppes Ltd). By the 1870s the company was also making ginger ale and 'Indian tonic water' by adding quinine to sweetened soda water, after the style of the British in India, who drank it as an antidote to malaria, thus beginning the fashion for gin and tonic. Schweppes merged with Cadbury Brothers Ltd in 1969, forming Cadbury Schweppes.

Wagon Wheel

A chocolate, biscuit and marshmallow sandwich named for its round shape – and because stories of the Wild West were very popular back when it was released in 1948.

Hairdressers with Punning Names

Although most London hairdressers are called something like 'Maison Roger', 'André' or 'Snippers', many have names that are clever puns on the service they offer. Here are 40 of them:

Alias Quiff & Combs
Ali Barber
Beyond the Fringe
Blow-Inn
Buzz-Bees
Curl Up & Dye
Cut Above
Cut Loose
Deb 'n' Hair
Do Yer Nut

Fringe Benefits
Hair & Now
Hairazors
Hair Today
Hair We Are
Hair We Go
Hairloom
Hairport
Hairs & Graces
Hats Off
Hazel Nutz
Head First
Headlines
Headmasters
Headway
Head Start
Heads We Do
Heads You Win
Heatwave
Lunatic Fringe
Mane Attraction
New Barnet
New Wave
Shear Pleasure
Shylocks
Streaks Ahead

Sun 'n' Hair
Swiss Hair
Uppercuts
Wavelength

Food Shops and Restaurants with Punning Names

A Salt & Battery
(Fish & chips)

Aesop's Tables
(Greek restaurant)

Brewed Awakening
(Coffee)

C'est Cheese
(Cheese)

The Codfather
(Fish and chips)

Frying Nemo
(Fish and chips)

The Frying Scotsman
(Fish and chips)

Grillers in the Mist
(Fish)

Jamaican Me Hungry
(Jamaican food)

Just Falafs
(Greek food)

Leaning Tower of Pizza
(Pizza)

Lettuce B. Frank
(Hot dogs)

Lettuce Eat
(Sandwiches)

Lord of the Fries
(Burgers and chips)

Meat You There
(Butcher's)

Melon Cauli
(Greengrocer's)

Men At Wok
(Chinese food)

Pete's A Place
(Pizza)

Pita Wrapbit
(Pittas and wraps)

Planet of the Grapes
(Wine)

Relish the Thought
(Sandwiches)

Thai Tanic
(Thai food)

Other Shops and Businesses with Punning Names

Cycloanalysts
(Bikes)

Floral 'n' Hardy
(Florists)

Frame, Set and Match
(Picture frames)

If Books Could Kill
(Mystery books)

Junk & Disorderly
(Junk shop)

The Merchant of Tennis
(Tennis equipment)

Napoleon Boiler Parts
(Plumber's)

New York Stocking Exchange
(Hosiery)

Once Upon a Crime
(Mystery books)

Optimeyes
(Optician's)

Pane in the Glass
(Glass repairs)

Sew What
(Tailoring)

Sofa So Good
(Furniture)

Sole-Man
(Shoe repairs)

Thistle Do Nicely
(Scottish souvenirs)

Wash Up Doc
(Launderette)

William the Concreter
(Concrete)

Inventions and Discoveries Named After People

Bakelite

Bakelite was an early form of plastic used extensively for products in the 1950s, and it takes its name from its creator – Belgian–American inventor Leo H. Baekeland (1863–1944).

Barbie Doll

The Barbie Doll was invented by American businesswoman Ruth Handler, the wife of one of the founders of the Mattel toy company, and named for their daughter Barbara. Realizing that most dolls of the time were representations of babies, Handler wanted to design one that could be dressed up like an adult. Despite initial scepticism at Mattel, the doll went on to be hugely successful.

Biro

On 10 June 1943 László József Bíró, a Hungarian sculptor, painter, hypnotist and journalist, patented the ballpoint pen that has ever since been known as the 'biro'. The idea of a ballpoint pen was not entirely new, but the invention as we know it came about only after many years of research, which began when László Bíró was a magazine editor and realized there would be a demand for a pen using the same quick-drying ink the printers used. With his brother Georg he developed a prototype featuring a rotating ball, and applied for patents in 1938. They abandoned their first idea – of using a piston to force the ink onto the tip – because ink seemed to squirt at random into the user's pocket, and instead hit upon a system involving capillary action in a tube. Biro ballpoints were first sold in Buenos Aires by the Eterpen Company in 1945, but the patents were later sold to the French company BiC (which owns the name 'Biro' as a trademark). László Bíró never made the fortune he deserved from his invention, and disappeared from public view.

Bloomers

Amelia Jenks Bloomer (1818–94) was the first woman editor of an American magazine, *The Lily*, and a supporter of the Women's Rights Movement who – somewhat ahead of her time – managed to persuade her husband to omit the word 'obey' from her marriage vows. She also supported 'dress reform' for women, in an attempt to free them from the tightly laced corsets and voluminous dresses then in fashion. The ensemble she proposed – which had in fact been designed and first worn by another dress reformer, Mrs Elizabeth Smith Miller – comprised a jacket and knee-length skirt beneath which a pair of trousers was worn tucked into boots. The outfit caused a storm of controversy. 'Bloomer girls' were refused entry to churches and other public buildings, while the *New York Herald* even went so far as to declare that 'Those who have tried it will very likely soon end their career in the lunatic asylum, or, perchance, in the State prison.' It was not long, however, before the 'bloomer dress' became popular on both sides of the Atlantic, particularly as a practical outfit for the newly popular pastime of bicycling, and the term 'bloomers' soon came to apply to just the trousers, or any sort of long undergarment.

Ferris Wheel

The first Ferris wheel was built at the Columbian Exposition in Chicago in 1893. It was designed by George Washington Gale Ferris (1859–96), an engineer from Galesburg, Illinois, who had entered a competition to design a structure that would rival the Eiffel Tower. It cost $385,000 to build and stood 76m high, with 36 cars, each capable of carrying up to 60 passengers. Ferris's original wheel operated until 1904, when it was moved to St Louis before being sold as scrap for just $1,800. In 1894 a Ferris wheel measuring a colossal 86.5m and capable of carrying 1,200 passengers in 40 cars (10 first-class and 30 second-class) was built in London for the Earls Court Exhibition.

Jacuzzi

The 'whirlpool bath' widely known as a jacuzzi is named after Candido Jacuzzi (1903–86), an Italian immigrant to the United States. His family was involved in aircraft production until 1921, when Giocondo, one of Candido's six brothers, died in a crash of a prototype monoplane. Following his death, their mother grounded the other brothers and urged them to make hydraulic pumps instead. Candido's son also happened to be crippled with rheumatoid arthritis, so he hit on the idea of using one of the firm's jet pumps for hydromassage, and the revolutionary bath was born. It started the cult of the hot tub, particularly in California, and was the basis of a multi–million dollar manufacturing empire.

Jeep

The name of this automobile comes partly from sounding out the initials 'GP' (General Purpose), but also from 'Eugene the Jeep', a character in the *Popeye* cartoon strip, whose powers were as remarkable as those of the military vehicle.

Leotard

Jules Léotard (1842–70), a successful French trapeze artist – and reputedly the first to turn a somersault in mid–air – was celebrated in his lifetime in the popular music-hall song, 'That

Daring Young Man on the Flying Trapeze'. After his death from smallpox at the early age of 28, his name lived on in the tight–fitting garment he invented for acrobats and dancers – which in the United States is often pluralized as 'leotards'.

Levi Jeans

Levi Strauss (1829–1902), a Bavarian immigrant, arrived in San Francisco in 1850 at the height of the Gold Rush that had started the previous year. The miners needed strong trousers, and Strauss began making them, firstly out of tent canvas, and later from denim, using copper rivets to reinforce the seams. The hard-wearing garment soon became standard clothing among cowboys, and following the revival of jeans during the 1960s, the company became one of the world's largest clothing manufacturers

Maverick

Samuel Augustus Maverick (1803–70), a wealthy Texan who owned the 385,000-acre Conquista Ranch near San Antonio, sold his herd of cattle to one A. Toutant Beauregard. As a large number of them had not been branded, they were indiscriminately rounded up by neighbouring ranchers, who branded them as their own, and by Beauregard's cowboys, who branded them as Maverick's – and maverick soon became the term used to describe any animal or person regarded as an outsider.

Salmonella

Because he was the first to identify it, Daniel Edward Salmon (1850–1914), an American veterinarian and US Department of Agriculture investigator, had the dubious honour of having the salmonella bacteria named after him.

Sideburns

American Union general Ambrose Everett Burnside (1824–81) started the fashion for side-whiskers. Perhaps because they were grown on the side of the face, their name was soon switched from burnsides to sideburns.

Stetson

John Batterson Stetson (1830–1906), a hatmaker born in New Jersey, established the John B. Stetson Manufacturing Company of Philadelphia, USA, which made the cowboy's famous '10–gallon' hat. It was often called a John B. before acquiring its better–known name of Stetson.

Teddy Bear

It is said that, while on a hunting trip, US president Theodore ('Teddy') Roosevelt refused to shoot a young bear. This became the subject of a famous cartoon by Clifford K. Berryman, published in the *Washington Post* on 16 November 1902. Immediately afterwards, Morris Michtom, a New York shopkeeper (and later founder of the Ideal Toy and Novelty Company), made stuffed bears and – with Roosevelt's permission – began advertising them as 'Teddy's Bears'.

At about the same time Margarete Steiff, a German toymaker, began making toy bears and exporting them to the USA to meet the demand 'Teddy's Bears' had created. Steiff bears, recognizable by their distinctive ear tags, are still made and are sold internationally, but the early examples are highly prized among collectors. All the most expensive bears ever sold at auction are Steiffs – including the world record holder, a bear of c.1920 sold at Sotheby's, London, on 19 September 1989 for £55,000.

Trilby Hat

The heroine of George du Maurier's novel Trilby, first published in 1894, was Trilby O'Ferrall, an artist's model who falls under the hypnotic spell of Svengali, a music teacher. The story recalls du Maurier's own days as an art student in Paris, and as he was both a writer and an artist, he illustrated the book himself, depicting his heroine in a soft felt hat. The novel was a huge success, and Trilby's name became attached to the headwear that soon became fashionable as a result.

Tureen

Henri, Vicomte de Turenne (1611–75), Marshal of France and commander of the French army during the Thirty Years War, once used his helmet as a soup bowl, hence giving the name 'tureen' to any large serving vessel – or so the story goes. A more likely explanation is that the word derives from *terrine*, French for an earthenware container.

Talk of the Town
Things Named After Towns

Many everyday items take their names from towns – usually the towns in which they were first used or created. Names like this are known as 'toponyms'. Here is a selection.

Academy

An institute of higher learning which takes its name from a school founded by ancient Greek philosopher Plato in Akademia, a sacred grove north of Athens.

Angora

Angora (currently known as Ankara) is the capital of Turkey, and gives its name to Angora cats, Angora goats, Angora

rabbits, and a type of wool made from the fur
of Angora rabbits.

Ascot Tie

A type of necktie with wide wings, historically worn at the
Ascot racecourse in Berkshire.

Badminton

The game of badminton, played with rackets and shuttlecocks,
was invented in about 1870 at Badminton House, the
Gloucestershire home of the Dukes of Beaufort. It spread
throughout the world, and in 1992 became an Olympic sport.
Badminton House has since become famous again as the
venue for an annual equestrian event.

Balaclava

Knitted headgear that exposes only part of the face, named for
the town of Balaklava in Crimea, Ukraine. In the Crimean War,
balaclavas were used by British troops to protect themselves
from the cold, and it is likely the name was coined then.

Bayonet

Legend says that peasants living in the French town of Bayonne
first stuck knives into the ends of their guns when they ran out
of powder and shot, thus turning them into primitive spears.

Bedlam

Bethlem Hospital, once known as Bedlam, is the oldest
psychiatric hospital in the world, and gives its name to the
word 'bedlam', meaning a state of uproar or confusion.

Bikini

The modern two-piece swimsuit is named after the Bikini Atoll
in the Pacific, although it was not invented there. In 1946 the

United States tested a nuclear bomb on the island, and the bikini's inventor was inspired to name his creation after the test.

Charleston

A dance of the 1920s popular in the city of Charleston, South Carolina, USA.

Clink

The Clink was a notorious medieval prison in Southwark, London, and its name went on to become a slang term for any prison.

Dollar

Silver was discovered in 1519 in St Joachimsthal in Germany ('thal' is a valley in German). The coins that were made there were called *thalers*, and when silver coins were first minted in the USA in 1794, the name became altered to dollars.

Duffel Coat/Bag

Coats made of a thick woollen material first made in the town of Duffel in Belgium. The material was originally used to make bags as well, although these days the word duffel bag can refer to any cylindrical bag with a drawstring.

Dungarees

The Indian region of Dongri made a type of coarse fabric that was often used in the production of these overalls, hence the name.

Geyser

A water spring that occasionally shoots large amounts of water into the air at great speed. The first one described by Europeans was Gersir in Iceland, and that name in turn comes from the Icelandic verb *geysa* – 'to gush'.

Jersey

A jumper named for Jersey, one of the Channel Islands, which has been famous for its knitting since medieval times.

Jodhpurs

Tight trousers usually worn for horse-riding, these were popularized in the 19th century as a style of clothing worn in northern India, and take their name from the city of Jodhpur.

Limousine

The women of Limousin in France wore hoods, the name of which was given to a type of carriage with a folding hood. Early cars were open, and the name was used for the first enclosed – and so more expensive and luxurious – cars.

Magenta

The bright crimson colour magenta is so called because the dye of this colour was discovered soon after the bloody (and hence red) battle fought at Magenta, Italy, in 1859.

Marathon

In 490 BC the news that the Athenians had defeated the Persians at the Battle of Marathon was carried by the messenger Pheidippides, who ran non-stop to Athens. Having done so, he dropped dead from exhaustion. At the first modern Olympics, held in Athens in 1896, runners covered the same route, from Marathon to Athens. The 26-mile 385-yard distance was established in 1924.

Neanderthal

A prehistoric subspecies related to the human race; remains were first discovered in Neanderthal (the valley of the Neander) in Germany.

Olympics

The modern Olympic Games have only been held since 1896, but the ancient Games they were based upon were supposedly first held in 776 BC at Olympia, Greece.

Rugby

Although the story itself is largely discredited, the legend says that a boy at Rugby School by the name of William Webb Ellis broke the rules of football by picking up the ball and running towards the goal. Even if the story is false, the legend has still attached the name of the town to the sport.

Serendipity

The act of making a fortunate discovery that you weren't expecting was coined by writer and politician Horace Walpole in reference to the Persian fairy tale 'The Three Princes of Serendip', in which the princes make similar lucky finds.

Siamese Twins

The condition of two identical twins whose bodies are joined, more correctly known as conjoined twins, is very rare. So rare that when two twins from Siam (now Thailand) known as Chang and Eng were born joined at the sternum, they were asked to tour the world and were promoted as the 'Siamese Twins' – the name becoming a term for the condition itself.

Spa

The Belgian town of Spa was famed for its springs, which people visited, bathed in and drank for their health. Other health resorts have since become known as spas.

Tarantula

The seaport of Taranto in Italy provided the name of the spider known as the tarantula. It was believed that a type of wild dancing that began in Taranto – the tarantella – was either caused by or was a cure for the bite of the spider.

Turkey

Turkeys were actually first encountered by Europeans in North America, but they were mistaken for a variety of guinea fowl, which were at that time imported from the country of Turkey, and the name stuck.

Football Club Nicknames

Many football clubs have unusual nicknames, often linked to the town in which they are based. Here is a list of some of the ones that might spark your imagination – if you think a match between Brentford (The Bees) and Bristol Rovers (The Pirates) might be quite exciting, then imagine what a match between actual bees and pirates might be like!

The Addicks

Charlton Athletic

A corruption of the word 'haddocks', named after a local fish-and-chip shop.

The Bantams

Bradford City

Considered lucky because of a myth of a bantam (a variety of poultry) getting on the team bus during the FA Cup-winning season of 1911.

The Bees

Brentford

Misinterpretation of an 1890s chant 'Buck up, Bs!'

The Black Cats

Sunderland

Named after the Black Cat battery gun on the bank of the river Wear, the site of the present stadium.

The Blades

Sheffield United

Sheffield is historically a centre of steel and cutlery production.

The Brewers
Burton Albion
Burton-on-Trent is linked to the brewing industry.

The Bulls
Hereford United
Named after a local breed of cattle.

The Canaries

Norwich City

Their home strip is yellow, and the bird is used in their logo.

The Cardinals

Woking

Their home kit is red, chosen because of the
town's links to Cardinal Wolsey.

The Chairboys

Wycombe Wanderers

The town is known for its furniture-making industry.

The Cobblers

Northampton Town

Famed for its shoe-making industry.

The Cottagers

Fulham

Named after the club's ground, Craven Cottage.

The Daggers

Dagenham & Redbridge

A shortening of part of the club name.

The Dolly Blues

Lancaster City

The team originally played in the same colour
as the Dolly Blue washing tablets.

The Eagles

Crystal Palace

These birds of prey are featured on the club's logo.

The Foxes
Leicester City
The county of Leicestershire is renowned for its many foxes.

The Glovers
Yeovil Town
Yeovil is known for its glove-making industry.

The Gunners
Arsenal
The club used to be based in Woolwich, near the site of the
Royal Arsenal, where guns were manufactured.

The Hatters
Luton Town/Stockport County
These clubs share a nickname, as they both have links to the
hat-making industry.

The Hornets (or the 'Orns)
Watford
Their strip is yellow and black, like a hornet.

The Imps
Lincoln City
From a legend about two imps being sent to Earth in the 14th
century to cause havoc and mayhem. One of them was turned
to stone in Lincoln Cathedral, and can still be seen there today.

The Irons
West Ham United
The team was originally called Thames Ironworks, and was
made up of employees of the works.

The Lambs
Tamworth
This team plays at the Lamb Ground, which is
named after a local pub.

The Lilywhites
Tottenham Hotspur
Their home strip is white – although they are more commonly
known as Spurs, a shortening of the name.

The Lions
Millwall
The name came about because of their reputation for giant-
killing (i.e. beating higher-ranked teams).

The Magpies
Newcastle United
Based on their black and white striped home shirts.

The Mariners
Grimsby Town
Grimsby is situated on the coast.

The Minstermen
York City
York Minster is one of the city's most famous landmarks.

The Monkeyhangers
Hartlepool United FC
During the Napoleonic Wars the citizens of Hartlepool
allegedly hanged a monkey because they thought
it was a French spy!

The Owls

Sheffield Wednesday

After they were presented with an owl mascot to honour their stadium at Owlerton.

The Pensioners

Chelsea

A 'Chelsea pensioner' is a name for someone who lives at the Royal Hospital, Chelsea, which is a retirement and nursing home for former members of the British army.

The Pilgrims

Boston United/Plymouth Argyle

These clubs are both based in places from where pilgrims set off to settle the lands of America.

The Pirates

Bristol Rovers

The town has historial links to shipping.

The Posh

Peterborough United

A former manager once proclaimed that he was looking for 'posh players for a posh new team'.

The Potters

Stoke City

The city is home to the pottery industry.

The Red Devils

Manchester United

This nickname was taken from nearby rugby league team Salford.

The Robins

*Cheltenham Town, Swindon Town, Bristol City,
Wrexham & Altrincham*

All these clubs play in red, like a robin's breast.

The Seasiders

Blackpool

Blackpool lies on the coast.

The Seagulls

Brighton & Hove Albion

These towns are by the sea, but the name is also a
response to the similar-sounding nickname
'The Eagles' of their arch-rivals Crystal Palace.

The Shakers

Bury

The club's first chairman, J. T. Ingham, said before a
Lancashire Cup game against Blackburn,
'We will shake them. In fact, we are the Shakers.'

The Shrimpers

Southend

Shrimping is historically a local industry.

The Spireites

Chesterfield

After the famous crooked spire of a church in the town.

The Swans

Swansea City

A shortened version of the name.

The Terriers

Huddersfield Town

Named after the Yorkshire terrier breed of dog.

The Tigers

Hull City/Gloucester City

Both clubs have an orange and black home strip.

The Toffees

Everton

Named after a local toffee shop that sold Everton Mints.

The Toon

Newcastle United

When the word 'town' is pronounced in a
Geordie accent, it sounds like 'toon'!

The Tractor Boys

Ipswich Town

Agriculture and farming are big industries in the region.

The Trotters

Bolton Wanderers

In the 19th century, one of the team's pitches was next to a
piggery and clearances often ended up in there. Players had to
'trot' through the pig-pens to retrieve the balls.

The Villans

Aston Villa

Just a shortening of the official name,
but it sounds intimidating all the same.

4. WAR
● ● ● ● ● ● ● ● ● ● ● ● ●
Weapons and Warfare

Big Bertha

The name given to the 142-ton cannon used by the German
army to shell Paris from a distance of 76 miles during the
First World War was derived from Bertha Krupp von Bohlen
und Halbach (1886–1957). She inherited the German Krupp
armaments business from her father Friedrich Alfred – who had
committed suicide in 1902. The name was originally given to
the army's much smaller howitzers – mistakenly, since they
were made by another firm, Skoda.

Bowie Knife

This large hunting knife was supposedly invented by Colonel
James Bowie (1796–1836), a Texan adventurer and slave trader
who died during the siege of the Alamo fortress by Mexican
soldiers, alongside his friend Davy Crockett. However, it has
been claimed that it was actually invented by his older brother
Rezin Pleasant Bowie (1793–1841). The lethal weapon,
jokingly called an 'Arkansas toothpick', had a blade 25–35cm
long, with a guard between the blade and the handle.

Browning Rifle

After John M. Browning (1854–1926), an American inventor.

Colt Revolver

Samuel Colt (1814–62), the revolver's American inventor, is
said to have whittled the original design in wood. Later, he
perfected a working version that was patented in England and
France in 1835 and in the United States the following year.

It was not immediately successful, but when the government ordered 1,000, the foundations were laid for what by 1855 was the world's largest gun factory. Colts were used extensively during the American Civil War, and the six-shot, single-action, .45-calibre Peacemaker model, introduced in 1873 (the classic six-gun), made Samuel Colt a wealthy man.

Derringer Pistol

The tiny pocket pistol was designed by Henry Deringer Jr of Philadelphia, USA (1786–1868). In 1865 John Wilkes Booth used a Deringer to assassinate US president Abraham Lincoln. In the following newspaper report, it was incorrectly spelled Derringer, with an extra 'r', and it is that spelling that has remained.

Gatling Gun

Dr Richard Jordan Gatling (1818–1903) patented his hand-cranked machine gun with a fire rate of up to 3,000 rounds per minute in 1862 – somewhat too late to be widely used in the American Civil War – and it was soon superseded by more efficient weapons.
The slang term 'gat' for any gun comes from the name.

Maxim Gun

Sir Hiram Stevens Maxim (1840–1916), US-born but a natural-ized British citizen, invented the gun in 1883 – as well as a flying machine, a mousetrap and many other gadgets.

Molotov Cocktail

A crude but effective petrol-filled bottle and fuse – dubbed a 'cocktail for Molotov' by Finns during the war against Russia (1940). Vyacheslav Mikhailovich Molotov (real name Skriabin; 1890–1986) was the Soviet prime minister at the time.

Shrapnel

The exploding shells were devised by British inventor
Lieutenant-General Henry Shrapnel (1761–1842) and used to
great effect in Wellington's defeat of Napoleon at Waterloo
in 1815. The name was later applied to any exploding
shell or bomb fragments.

Sten Gun

The name comes from the first letters of the names of the
weapon's inventors, Major R. V. Shepherd and H. J. Turpin,
combined with the first two letters of England (or, according to
some authorities, Enfield), where it was first made (in 1940).

Tommy Gun

Invented by American army general John Taliaferro
Thompson (1860–1940) and navy commander John
Bell Blish (1860–1921), the Thompson sub-machine
gun became known as the 'Tommy gun' – particularly
when it was used by gangsters during the 1920s.

Winchester Rifle

Oliver Fisher Winchester (1810–80) was an American gunmak-
er who gave his name to the Winchester Repeating
Arms Company, manufacturers of the rifle most used by
cowboys – the Model 73 Winchester Repeater.

I Name This Ship . . .

British Warship Nicknames

Her Majesty's ships are always given nicknames by
their crews. These are deliberate humorous mispronunciations
of the proper names – and often show more than a bit
of gallows humour!

Aggie
HMS Agamemnon

Aggie on Horseback
HMS Weston-Super-Mare

Named after Agnes Weston, a campaigner in the temperance movement and for sailors' welfare. 'On horseback' is a light-hearted mistranslation of the Latin super-mare (on the sea) – 'mare' being a female horse.

'Am and Tripe
HMS Amphitrite

Humorous mispronunciation.

Archdeacon
HMS Venerable

A play on the phrase 'venerable archdeacon'.

Billy Ruffian
HMS Bellerophon

Century One
HMS Centurion

Christmas Anthem
HMS Chrysanthemum

Cocoa Boat
HMS Curacoa

Curious
HMS Furious

Despair Ship Remorse

HMS Resource

Humorous mispronunciation of 'repair ship Resource'.

Dreado

HMS Dreadnought

Eggshells

HMS Achilles

Exploder

HMS Explorer

This experimental submarine was fitted with a dangerous hydrogen peroxide propulsion system!

The Fighting G

HMS Gloucester

Flatiron

HMS Argus

From the shape of the ship.

Gin Palace

HMS Agincourt

Originally built for the Brazilian navy and so named as it had higher standards of comfort, particularly for officers, than most Royal Navy ships.

The Golden Devil

HMS Sovereign of the Seas

He-Cat

HMS Hecate

HMS Refit
HMS Renown

HMS Repair
HMS Repulse

The Lord's Own
HMS Vengeance

Derived from the phrase 'the Lord's own vengeance'
(based on the Bible, Romans 12:19)

Maggie
HMS Magnificent/HMCS Magnificent

The Mighty Hood
HMS Hood

Nelly
HMS Nelson

Niffy Jane
HMS Iphigenia

Northo
HMS Northumberland

The Old Lady
HMS Warspite

*Admiral of the Fleet Viscount Cunningham once
commented about the ship's speed: 'When the old
lady lifts her skirts she can run.'*

One-Eye
HMS Polyphemus
Polyphemus was a cyclops in Greek mythology.

Outrageous
HMS Courageous

The Pool
HMS Liverpool

Puffington
HMS Effingham

Rezzo
HMS Resolution

Rusty-guts
HMCS Restigouche

Shiny Sheff
HMS Sheffield

The Smoke
HMS London

Spurious
HMS Furious

Tea Boat
HMS Ceylon

Tea Chest
HMS Thetis

Tiddly Quid
HMS Royal Sovereign

Tin Duck
HMS Iron Duke

The Toothless Terror
HMS Scylla

Traffie
HMS Trafalgar

Uproarious
HMS Glorious

British Regimental Nicknames

The Agile and Suffering Highlanders
Argyll and Sutherland Highlanders

The Bengal Tigers
South Wales Borderers

Bingham's Dandies
17th Lancers

The Bloodsuckers
63rd Regiment of Foot

The Bogging Royals
Royal Scots

The Borg
Royal Green Jackets

The Brickdusts
53rd Regiment of Foot

The Cat and Cabbage
York and Lancaster Regiment

The Cauliflowers
47th Regiment of Foot

The Cherry Pickers
11th Hussars

The Death or Glory Boys
17th Lancers

The Desert Rats
7th Armoured Division

The Dirty Half-hundred
50th Regiment of Foot

The Dirty Shirts
101st Regiment of Foot (later Royal Munster Fusiliers)

The Donkey Wallopers
Household Cavalry

The Eagle Catchers
Royal Scots Greys; Royal Scots Dragoon Guards

The Emperor's Chambermaids
14th King's Hussars

The Eversworded
29th Regiment of Foot

The First and Worst
Royal Scots

The Fore and Aft
Royal Gloucestershire Regiment

The Gay Gordons
Gordon Highlanders

The Granny-knotters
Staffordshire Regiment

The Grasshoppers
95th Regiment of Foot

The Havercake Lads
33rd Regiment of Foot; Duke of Wellington's Regiment, previously 1st Yorkshire West Riding Regiment

Hickety Pip
65th Regiment of Foot

The Holy Boys
9th Regiment of Foot

The Immortals
76th Regiment of Foot

The Ladies from Hell
Black Watch

The Leather Hats
8th (King's) Regiment of Foot

The Monkeys
Royal Military Police

The Mutton Lancers
Queen's (Royal West Surrey) Regiment

Nobody's Own
20th Hussars

The Old Farmers
5th Royal Inniskilling Dragoon Guards

The Old Seven and Sixpennies
76th Regiment of Foot

The Orange Lilies
35th Regiment of Foot

The Nutcrackers
3rd Regiment of Foot

Paupers Horse
13th/18th Hussars

The Pigs
76th Regiment of Foot

The Poachers
2nd Battalion, Royal Anglian Regiment

The Poison Dwarves
The Cameronians

The Pompadours
3rd Battalion, Royal Anglian Regiment

Pontius Pilate's Bodyguard
1st Regiment of Foot; Royal Scots

The Resurrectionists
3rd Regiment of Foot

The Royal Tigers
65th (2nd Yorkshire, North Riding) Regiment of Foot

Sankey's Horse
39th (Dorsetshire) Regiment of Foot

The Saucy Sixth
6th Regiment of Foot

The Tangerines
2nd Regiment of Foot

The Tots
17th Lancers

The Ups and Downs
Welsh Regiment, 96th Regiment of Foot

The Vikings
1st Battalion Royal Anglian Regiment

The Vulgar Fraction
16th/5th Queen's Royal Lancers

The Yeller Bellies
10th Regiment of Foot, Lincolnshire Regiment

The Young and Lovelies
84th (York and Lancaster) Regiment of Foot

5. TRANSPORT
• • • • • • • • • • • • • • •

Airports Named After People

John Lennon Airport

Liverpool

Musician with The Beatles (1940–80)

Robin Hood Airport

Doncaster/Sheffield

Character from English legend

George Best Belfast City Airport

Belfast

Footballer for Northern Ireland and Manchester United
(1946–2005)

Charles M. Schulz Airport

Sonoma County, California, USA

Cartoonist, creator of Snoopy *and* Peanuts *(1922–2000)*

John F. Kennedy International Airport

New York, USA

35th president of the USA (1917–1963)
He also has airports named after him in Ashland, Wisconsin,
USA, and in La Paz, Bolivia.

John Wayne Airport

Orange County, California, USA

Actor (1907–79)

Charles De Gaulle Airport

Paris, France

Former president of France (1890–1970)

George Bush Intercontinental Airport

Houston, Texas

41st president of the USA (1924–)

Leonardo da Vinci/Fiumicino Airport

Rome, Italy

Italian artist and scientist (1452–1519)

Louis Armstrong New Orleans International Airport

New Orleans, Louisiana, USA

Jazz musician (1901–71)

Galileo Galilei Airport

Pisa, Italy

Italian astronomer and scientist (1564–1642)

Marco Polo Airport
Venice, Italy
Venetian explorer (c.1254–1324)

Indiana County/Jimmy Stewart Airport
Indiana, Pennsylvania, USA
Actor (1908–1997)

Queen Beatrix International Airport
Oranjestad, Aruba
Queen of the Netherlands (1938–)

W. A. Mozart Airport
Salzburg, Austria
Composer (1756–1791)

W. K. Kellogg Regional Airport
Battle Creek, Michigan, USA
Founder of Kellogg's cereal manufacturers (1860–1951)

Cars That Are Named After People

The following car models and companies are all named after people – usually the founders of the company.

Alfa Romeo

Italy, *Nicola Romeo* (1876–1938)

Armstrong Siddeley

UK, *William George Armstrong* (1810–1900)
& *John Davenport Siddeley* (1866–1953)

Audi

Germany, *August Horch* (1868–1951), whose surname
means 'hark' in German, which in Latin is *audi*.

Austin

UK, *Herbert Austin* (1866–1941)

Bentley

UK, *Walter Owen Bentley* (1888–1971)

Bugatti

Italy, *Ettore Bugatti* (1881–1947)

Cadillac

USA, *Antoine Laumet de La Mothe, sieur de Cadillac* (1658–
1730) – ancestor of *Henry M. Leland*, founder of the company

Chevrolet

USA, *Louis Chevrolet* (1878–1941)

Chrysler

USA, *Walter Chrysler* (1875–1940)

Daimler
Germany, *Gottlieb Daimler* (1834–1900)

Dodge
USA, *Horace Dodge* (1868–1920) and
John Francis Dodge (1864–1920)

Edsel
USA, produced by Ford, named after founder
Henry Ford's son *Edsel Bryant Ford* (1893–1943).

Ferrari
Italy, *Enzo Ferrari* (1898–1988)

Ford
USA, *Henry Ford* (1863–1947)

Honda
Japan, *Soichiro Honda* (1906–1991)

Lamborghini
Italy, *Ferruccio Elio Arturo Lamborghini* (1916–1993)

Lancia
Italy, *Vincenzo Lancia* (1881–1937)

Lincoln
USA, *President Abraham Lincoln* (1809–1865)

Maserati
Italy, *Maserati Brothers* (*Carlo* (1881–1910), *Bindo* (1883–
1980), *Alfieri II* (1887–1932), *Mario* (1890–1981),
Ettore (1894–1990) and *Ernesto* (1898–1975)

Mercedes-Benz

Germany, *Mercédès Jellinek* (1889–1929), the
daughter of Austrian automobile entrepreneur *Emil Jellinek*,
who named a series of cars in her honour, and
Karl Benz (1844–1929), the founder

Peugeot

France, *Armand Peugeot* (1849–1915)

Porsche

Germany, *Ferdinand Oliver Porsche* (1961–)

Renault

France, *Louis Renault* (1877–1944), *Marcel Renault*
(1872–1903) and *Fernand Renault* (1863–1909)

Rolls-Royce

UK, *Charles Rolls* (1877–1910) and *Henry Royce* (1863–1933)

Skoda

Czechoslovakia, *Emil Škoda* (1839–1900), founder of Škoda
Works arms manufacturer, which later turned to making cars.

Toyota

Japanese, *Kiichiro Toyoda* (1894–1952)

Brighton Bus Names

Since 1999 the Brighton and Hove Bus Company
have been naming their buses after famous people
who have a connection to the area. Here is a selection:

1. Lord Attenborough (1923–)

Actor and film director
(No longer in service)

3. Norman Cook (1963–)

Musician
(No longer in service)

4. Chris Eubank (1966–)

Boxer
(No longer in service)

8. Sally Gunnell (1966–)

Olympic hurdler
(No longer in service)

19. The Who (1964–)

Rock band
(No longer in service)

801. King Charles II (1630–85)

Former king of England

808. Rudyard Kipling (1865–1936)

Author of The Jungle Book

*(No longer in service due to a de-roofing accident; it was
converted to an open-top bus for sightseeing tours and
renamed Henry Allingham, 869)*

817. Lord Olivier (1907–1989)
Actor

825. Sir Winston Churchill (1874–1965)
British prime minister

828. Charles Dickens (1812–70)
Author

887. Virginia Woolf (1882–1941)
Author of *To the Lighthouse*

916. Ben Sherman (1925–87)
Clothing producer

Named Trains

The Flying Dutchman
A service that ran in the west of England between 1849 and 1892, and which was named after a famous racehorse of the day.

The Flying Scotsman
A passenger train that has run from London to Edinburgh along the east coast since 1862.

The Golden Arrow
A train which ran from London to Dover to connect with ferries to Paris. It ran from 1926 to 1972, with a gap for the Second World War.

The Green Arrow
Built in 1936 for the London and North Eastern Railway.

The Mallard

Built in 1938, and the world record holder for
fastest steam locomotive.

The Night Ferry

This train service was the only one to convey passengers
across the Channel to France before the opening of the
Channel Tunnel. It travelled from London to Dover, where it
was split into sections so it could be placed on a ferry without
upsetting the balance, before being reassembled on the other
side to continue its journey to Paris.

Puffing Billy

Constructed between 1813 and 1814, this is the world's oldest
surviving steam locomotive.

Stephenson's Rocket (1829)

Constructed in 1829 for the Rainhill Trials – a competition to
see what kind of locomotive would operate on the Liverpool
and Manchester Railway. The rocket, with an average speed of
12 mph, won the competition.

Wylliam Dilly

Built in 1815, and thought for a while to be the oldest steam
locomotive in the world, until examinations revealed it com-
tained improvements on Puffing Billy's design, and so must
have been constructed afterwards.

And Spong . . . ?

● ● ● ● ● ● ● ● ● ● ● ● ● ●

So that brings us to the end of this guide to the names of places, people and things – but did you spot *Boring*, *Botty* and *Spong*?

Boring is a town in Oregon, and can be found in the 'Places' section under 'Misleading Place Names'.

Botty can be found in the 'People' section as both an unusual first name and an unusual surname.

But what about *Spong*? Eagle-eyed readers might have spotted it in the unusual surnames list, as it is a rare surname which comes from an Old English word for 'a narrow strip of land'. But if it's the title of the 'Things' section, then shouldn't it be the name of a thing as well as a person?

It is also the name of a company established in 1856 at the age of 16 by James Osborn Spong under his family name. It became one of Britain's biggest manufacturers of kitchen equipment and other household goods such as mincers, knife polishers, coffee mills and fire extinguishers, and patented many gadgets. The company went out of business in the 1980s, so you might find it a little hard to find any Spong kitchen equipment today, but ask your parents – you never know how long some of their stuff has been hanging around!

GLOSSARY

● ● ● ● ● ● ● ● ● ● ● ● ● ● ●

Acronym A word made from the initial letters of other words: *scuba* (self-contained underwater breathing apparatus)

Allonym A person's name adopted by someone else, such as a writer

Ananym A name written backwards: Samuel Butler's 1872 novel *Erehwon*, which is 'nowhere' spelled backwards

Anepronym A trademark that has become the common name for the product: *aspirin* or *hoover*

Anonym Another word for pseudonym

Appellation The name by which something or someone is known

Aptronym A name that that is appropriate for its owner or his job: the *Mr Men* characters Mr Tickle, Mr Happy and Mr Messy

Astronym The name of a star, galaxy, etc.

Autonym A writer's real name; work published under a writer's own name (*see pseudonym*)

Clepe An old-fashioned word for 'name'

Cognomen In ancient Rome, a nickname that over time became a hereditary family name

Comiconomenclaturist A person who collects humorous names such as aptronyms

Cryptonym A secret or code name: 'the Manhattan Project' – the United States' programme to build an atomic bomb

Demonym The name of the residents of a place: Liverpudlian, Mancunian

Diminutive The short version of a person's name: *Alex* for Alexander, *Nick* for Nicholas

Eponym A name from which another name is derived: the biro, named after its inventor László Bíró

Euonym A beautiful name

Exonym The name of a place in a foreign language: *L'Angleterre* is the French exonym of England

Geonym The name of a geographic feature

Hodonym The name of a street or road: Broadway in New York or Princes Street in Edinburgh

Hydronym The name of river, lake, etc: the river Severn

Jobonym A name that is appropriate to a person's job: Sir Ronald Brain, brain surgeon

Metronym A name taken from the mother's name

Mononym The name of a person known by a single name: the singer Madonna

Namephreak Another word for aptronym

Necronym The name of a person who has died, sometimes given to a new child in their memory

Nomen An ancient Roman's second name

Odonym Another word for the name of a street or road

Oeconym The name of a house or building: the White House or the Albert Hall

Onomasticon A list or book of names of people and places: like *Boring, Botty and Spong!*

Onomastics The study of proper names and their origins

Onomatology Another word for onomastics

Onymous A book that has its author's name – the opposite of anonymous

Oronym The name of a hill or mountain: Ben Nevis

Paedonymic A name derived from that of one's child

Patronym A name derived from one's father's name

Phytonym The name of a plant: daffodil, rose bush

Praenomen An ancient Roman's first or given name

Proper name The name of a person or place, usually spelled with a capital letter: Russell Ash

Pseudonym The fictitious name used by an author: the author Lemony Snicket, real name Daniel Handler

Tautonym A name where both first and surname are the same

Teknonymy Referring to a parent by the name of its child: 'John's mother'

Theonym A name for a god: Yahweh or Zeus

Toponym A place name or the name of something based on a place name

Toponymy The study of place names

Zoonym The name of an animal: cat, dog, star-nosed mole

In memory of Russell Ash
18th June 1946–21st June 2010